D1498722

RELIGIOUS POETRY AND PROSE OF JOHN DONNE

Religious Poetry and Prose

John Donne

Edited and Mildly Modernized by
HENRY L. CARRIGAN, JR.

PARACLETE PRESS
BREWSTER, MASSACHUSETTS

Library of Congress Cataloging-in-Publication Data

Donne, John, 1572-1631.
     [Selections. 1999]
     Religious poetry and prose/ John Donne; edited and mildly
modernized by Henry L. Carrigan, Jr.
          p.   cm.
     ISBN 1-55725-235-1 (pbk.)
     1. Spiritual life—Christianity. 2. Christian life—Church of England.
I. Carrigan, Henry L., 1954- II. Title.
     BV4501.2 .D6365 1999
     242—dc21   99-34592
                                                                CIP

10   9   8   7   6   5   4   3   2   1

© 1999 by Paraclete Press
ISBN 1-55725-235-1

All rights reserved. No part of this book may be reproduced in any form
or by any means without the prior written consent of the publisher, except
in brief quotations used in reviews.

Published by Paraclete Press
Brewster, Massachusetts
www.paraclete-press.com

Printed in the United States of America.

Contents

Introduction

Although many readers may not be aware of it, most of us are familiar with John Donne's words because they have been used in the titles of a number of classic novels and autobiographies. Ernest Hemingway's novel *For Whom the Bell Tolls* takes its title from Donne's famous Meditation 17, where the poet, in an oft-repeated phrase, declares, "No man is an island, entire of itself; every man is a piece of the continent, a part of the main[land]. . . . Any man's death diminishes me, because I am involved in mankind, and therefore never know for whom the bell tolls; it tolls for you." And John Gunther's poignant autobiography of separation and loss, *Death Be Not Proud*, draws its title from one of Donne's Holy Sonnets. In fact, many phrases taken from Donne's Holy Sonnets—"Batter my heart, three person'd God"; "I am a little world made cunningly"—are familiar to readers, though they may not be aware that the words are Donne's.

Perhaps the most influential of all English poets, John Donne challenged the conventions of Elizabethan poetry, introducing a poetic style that later came to be called "metaphysical." Such poetry often addressed itself to the intellect, engaging in intellectual wordplay and ingenious comparison. In his poem "The Flea," for instance, Donne uses the flea as the image of both the marriage bed and the Holy Trinity. Metaphysical poetry is also personally passionate, attempting to unite both thought and feeling. Such poetry values above all, wit and paradox, irony and ambiguity, and Donne's poetry as well as his religious writings embrace and reflect these values. Although Donne had contemporary critics— the poet Ben Jonson said that because Donne did not observe Elizabethan poetic convention he "deserved hanging"—his poetic style greatly influenced T.S. Eliot as well as a number of literary critics who taught that irony and paradox were the supreme values of poetry.

John Donne belonged to a time marked by theological controversy as well as a time rich in the literature of worship, liturgy, and devotion. When *The Book of Common Prayer* appeared in 1549, its form and style influenced Donne's devotional writings as well as those of many others. Indeed, other poets such as George Herbert and Robert Herrick, both contemporaries of Donne, produced poems abounding in religious imagery. The sermons of Richard Hooker and Lancelot Andrewes, the devotional writing of Jeremy Taylor, and the meditative writings of Sir Thomas Browne also appeared during Donne's life. A seminal event was the appearance of the King James Version of the Bible in 1611. For the first time, a wide number of lay people had an opportunity to read the Bible themselves, in their language, rather than hearing the Latin Bible read to them by Roman Catholic priests. These cultural conditions contributed to the beauty and ardor of Donne's religious writings.

Biography

John Donne was born in London in 1572 to Roman Catholic parents. His father, before his death in 1576, was the Warden of the Company of Ironmongers, and therefore was a prominent citizen of London. Donne's mother, Elizabeth Haywood, was descended from an eminent Roman Catholic family; two of Elizabeth's brothers were Jesuits, and one of them, Jasper, was imprisoned and sentenced to condemnation in the Tower of London in 1583 for being a Jesuit missionary to the Anglicans of England. The effect of his uncle's imprisonment likely had an effect on Donne, though he later wrote one treatise, *Ignatius his Conclave* (1611), in which he attacked the Jesuits. Thus, in an increasingly powerful Anglican England, Donne and family were nonconformists.

When Donne was eleven years old, he enrolled in Oxford, circumventing Oxford's requirement that all registering students over the age of sixteen acknowledge the supremacy of the crown over the Church. Donne, who because of his Catholicism was loyal to the Pope and could not announce his allegiance to the crown, entered the university early and completed his education by 1589, at the age of 17. We possess little information about Donne's Oxford career other than that it followed the classic medieval curriculum of rhetoric and theology.

From 1592 to 1594, Donne studied law at Lincoln's Inn. Many date his concern with religion and religious controversy to this period. In 1593, Donne was greatly affected by the imprisonment and death of his younger brother, Henry. Arrested when his school's officials discovered a Roman Catholic priest in his rooms, Henry later died in prison of the plague. Donne's brother's death, his growing skepticism, and his close examination of the religious controversies of his day contributed to his gradual turn from Roman Catholicism to Anglicanism.

Although the Lincoln's Inn years were marked by this religious turn, they also marked the period in Donne's life when he turned away from things religious to more worldly entertainments. He frequented taverns and theaters and became an ardent lover of beautiful women. It was during this period that he established a growing reputation as a poet of verse letters, love poems, and satires.

Between 1596 and 1597, Donne served briefly in the military service of the Earl of Essex before becoming the secretary to Sir Thomas Egerton, who presided over the Upper House of Parliament. During his years of service to Egerton, Donne's reputation as a wit, a poet, and a womanizer continued to grow.

In 1600, Donne met and fell in love with Ann More, a girl of fourteen and a niece of Queen Elizabeth. Because of his reputation as a womanizer and a writer of risqué love verses, Donne could not hope to get Ann's father's blessing to marry her. So the two met in London and married in secret. When Ann's father discovered this secret marriage, he threw Donne in prison for marrying a minor. Donne lost his position with Egerton, who refused to give him any financial support. Through letters he pleaded with More for forgiveness, and More finally had Donne released, but he refused to promise Donne any financial assistance.

For the next thirteen years, Donne and Ann lived in semipoverty, seeking assistance, and receiving it most of the time, from Donne's wealthy friends. During these years Ann bore five children, and Donne began to experience a series of bouts with ill health. In 1606, the couple moved to Mitcham, near London, and it was during this period at Mitcham that he wrote much of his religious verse, including "A Litany," "La Corona (The Crown)," and most of his "Holy Sonnets." In 1610, Donne wrote *Pseudo-Martyr*, a treatise in which he tried to persuade ambivalent Roman Catholics to declare their allegiance to King James I. This treatise was very popular, and King James urged him to consider ordination. Although Donne's religious sensibility continued to deepen during this period, he was still enamored of worldly glory and, to that end, continued to seek an appointment at court, putting off any thoughts of ordination. In 1611, he accepted the wealthy patronage of Sir Robert Drury and wrote the *Anniversaries* in memory of Drury's daughter, Elizabeth.

Between 1611 and 1615, Donne's fortunes reached a low ebb. Ann and all five of his children became very ill, and Donne himself almost went blind. In addition, his finances were in ruin. During these four years he studied Hebrew and Greek, as if he were preparing to enter the priesthood. Continuing to write, in 1614 he completed the *Essays in Divinity*, a set of biblical interpretations that followed the traditional four-fold method of scriptural interpretation.

Donne's fortunes took a turn for the better after his ordination on January 23, 1615. His first appointment was as Chaplain-in-Ordinary to the King and he was then made Doctor of Divinity at Cambridge. Late in 1616, Donne was appointed as Divinity Reader of Lincoln's Inn. We possess twenty-eight of the sermons he preached while he was there. In 1617, Ann died, and following her death, Donne's sense of his religious vocation grew deeper. Donne wrote "Hymn to Christ, at the Author's Last Going in to Germany" as a reflection of his increasing anxiety on accompanying James Hay, a chaplain on mission to Germany, to that country.

On November 22, 1621, Donne was installed as Dean of St. Paul's Cathedral, London, where he was to remain the rest of his life. Over the next decade, Donne experienced bouts of serious illness, including a bout of "relapsing fever," which leaves the patient mentally alert but physically weak. Donne wrote his *Devotions upon Emergent Occasions* while he recuperated from this illness. In addition, he wrote "Hymn to God the Father" and "Hymn to God my God, in my Sickness" during this time. Although he remained active in reading, writing, and preaching, by 1630 Donne was so ill that he had to leave London for the country. He returned to London on the first Friday in Lent to preach what he called "the author's own funeral sermon," "Death's Duel." Donne died on March 31, 1631.

Religious Writings

Although the majority of Donne's religious writings come from the later period of his life, many of them contain an implicit concern for things religious. Even so ribald a lyric as "The Flea," Donne's meditation upon the marriage bed, is intertwined with his reflection upon the ways that the Trinity is reflected in a marital relationship. But his more mature reflections on religion do indeed belong to his later years.

Donne's religious writings express a clearly incarnational theology. The Incarnation, the Atonement, and the Resurrection are the central themes of his sermons. His Christmas and Easter sermons are passionate and fiery paeans to the love of Christ. Even his Trinity sermons focus on the powerful and overwhelming love of Christ. This wonder and awe at the love of God incarnate in Christ also emerges from his *Devotions* and the *Essays in Divinity*.

Donne's religious poetry also communicates the power of Christ's love to weak sinners. Reflecting Donne's constant awareness of the sins of his early life, his poems often express his unworthiness to be forgiven by God in Christ. Revealing Donne's emphasis on Christ's earthly ministry, the first cycle of the Holy Sonnets traces Jesus' life and work from the Annunciation to the Ascension, and explored the ways that his life and work affect ours.

Donne's illnesses also loom large in his poetry and his prose. In the *Devotions* and in his prayers, physical illness often serves as a metaphor for spiritual illness. His great anxiety and despair about death are assuaged only by Christ's having delivered us from death by his own death, a point Donne makes with one repeated force in "Death's Duel." His fear of death, even though it may be found in such early poems as "A Valediction: forbidding Mourning," occupies much of his religious poetry as, for example, in "Hymn to God my God, in my Sickness." Donne's greatest hope, even in illness and anticipation of death, is the mysterious love of God in Christ, who has delivered us from death and has gone to prepare a place for us in God's kingdom. Donne's religious writings are as full of thought and passion, irony and paradox, as his worldly writings.

A Word About the Text

I have selected several of Donne's religious writings that I believe have a deep impact upon the spiritual life. I have not included his more explicitly theological writings from the *Essays* in *Divinity*, nor have I included selections from his more polemical writings such as *Ignatius his Conclave*.

I have drawn the selections here from several earlier editions. For the poetry I have used H.J.C. Grierson's standard *Donne's Poetical Works*, v.1, London: Oxford University Press, 1912. I drew the selected passages from Donne's sermons from Logan Pearsall Smith, *Donne's Sermons: Selected Passages*, London: Oxford at the Clarendon Press, 1919. "Death's Duel" and many of the prayers in this book I have drawn from *Devotions Upon Emergent Occasions, Together with Death's Duel*, Ann Arbor: University of Michigan Press, 1959. Finally, I have used *Essays in Divinity by John Donne*, edited by Evelyn M. Simpson, London: Oxford at the Clarendon Press, 1952.

I have tried to remain true to the spirit of Donne's texts even where I have mildly modernized them. I have replaced archaic words and forms of address with more modern ones. Thus, "thou" becomes "you" throughout. I have altered the syntax and sentence structure of the writing to make it livelier and more appealing to a contemporary audience. Most often this simply means casting sentences in the active rather than the passive voice. I have not always altered the syntax of the poetry, preferring to preserve Donne's poetic structure.

Henry L. Carrigan, Jr.
Westerville, Ohio

CHAPTER I
Divine Poems

Holy Sonnets

1. *The Crown*
   Deign at my hands this crown of prayer and praise,
   Weaved in my low devout melancholy,
   You which of good, have, yes are treasury,
   All changing unchanged Ancient of days;
   But do not, with a vile crown of frail bays,
   Reward my muse's white sincerity,
   But what your thorny crown gained, that give to me,
   A crown of glory, which always flowers;
   The ends crown our works, but you crown our ends,
   For, at our end begins our endless rest;
   The first last end, now zealously possessed,
   With a strong sober thirst, my soul attends.
   Salvation to all whose will is near.

2. *Annunciation*
   Salvation to all whose will is near;
   That All, which always is All everywhere,
   Which cannot sin, and yet all sins must bear,
   Which cannot die, yet cannot choose but to die,
   Lo, faithful Virgin, he yields himself to lie
   In prison, in your womb; and though he there
   Can take no sin, nor you give him sin, yet he will wear
   Taken from you, flesh, which death's force may try.

Before the sphere's time was created, you
Were in his mind, who is your Son, and Brother;
Whom you conceive, conceived; yes, you are now
Your Maker's maker, and your Father's mother;
You have light in dark; and shut in little room,
Immensity cloistered in your dear womb.

3. *Nativity*

Immensity cloistered in your dear womb,
Now leaves his beloved imprisonment,
There he has made himself to his intent
Weak enough, now into our world to come;
But Oh, for you, for him, has the inn no room?
Yet lay him in this stall, and from the Orient,
Stars, and wise men will travel to prevent
The effect of Herod's jealous general doom.
Do you see, my soul, with your faith's eyes, how he
Which fills all place, yet none holds him, does lie?
Was not his pity toward you wondrous,
That would have need to be pitied by you?
Kiss him, and with him into Egypt go,
With his kind mother, who partakes of your woe.

4. *Temple*

With his kind mother who partakes of your woe,
Joseph turn back; see where your child sits,
Blowing out those sparks of wit,
Which he himself on the Doctors did bestow;
The Word but lately could not speak, and lo,
It suddenly speaks wonders; about where it comes from,
And how does it happen
That all which was, and all which should be written,
A shallow seeming child should deeply know?
His Godhead was not soul to his manhood,

Nor had time mellowed to this ripeness,
But as for one who has a long task, it is good,
With the Sun to begin his business,
He in his age's morning thus began
By miracles exceeding the power of man.

5. *Crucifying*

By miracles exceeding the power of man,
He begat faith in some, envy in others,
For, what weak spirits admire, the ambitious hate;
In both affections many ran to him,
But Oh! The worst are most, they will and can,
Alas, and do, unto the immaculate,
Whose creature Fate is, now prescribe a fate,
Measuring self-life's infinity to a span,
To an inch. Lo, where condemned he
Bears his own cross, with pain, yet by and by
When it bears him, he must bear more and die.
Now you are lifted up, draw me to you,
And at your death giving such liberal dole,
Moisten, with one drop of your blood, my dry soul.

6. *Resurrection*

Moisten, with one drop of your blood, my dry soul
Shall (though she now be in extreme degree
Too stony and hard, and yet too fleshly) be
Freed by that drop, from being starved, hard, or foul,
And life, by this death bled, shall control
Death, whom your death slew; nor shall to me
Fear of first or last death, bring misery,
If in your little book my name you enroll,
Flesh in that long sleep is not putrified,
But made that there, of which, and for which it was;
Nor can by any other means be glorified.

May then sins sleep, and deaths soon pass from me,
That woke up from both, that risen I may again
Salute the last, and everlasting, day.

7.   *Ascension*

Salute the last, and everlasting, day,
Joy at the rising of the Sun, and Son,
You whose just tears, or tribulation
Have purely washed, or burned your drossy clay;
Behold the Highest, now parting from here,
Lightens the dark clouds he treads upon,
Nor does he, by ascending, show alone,
But first he, and he first, enters the way.
O strong Ram, which has battered heaven for me,
Mild Lamb, whose blood has marked my path;
Bright Torch that shines for me to see my way,
Oh, with your own blood quench your own just wrath,
And if your Holy Spirit my Muse did raise,
Deign at my hands this crown of prayer and praise.

8.   (I)

You have made me. Shall your work decay?
Repair me now, for my end comes quickly,
I run toward death and death runs toward me,
And all my pleasures are like yesterday.
I dare not move my dim eyes in any direction,
Despair behind, and death before cast
Such terror, and my feeble flesh so wastes away
By the sin in it, that it weighs toward hell.
Only you are above, and when I can look toward you,
I rise again.
But our old subtle foe so tempts me
That I cannot sustain myself for one hour.

Your grace may wing me to prevent his art,
And you will draw my iron heart toward you like a magnet.

9. (II)

As due by many titles I resign
Myself to you, O God, first I was made
By you, and for you, and when I was decayed,
Your blood bought that which was yours.
I am your son, made with yourself to shine,
Your servant, whose pains you have still repaid.
Your sheep, your Image, and, till I betrayed
Myself, a temple of your Holy Spirit.
Why does the devil usurp me?
Why does he steal, even ravish, which is your right?
Unless you rise and fight for your own work,
I shall soon despair, when I do see
That you love humanity so well, yet will not choose me,
And Satan hates me, yet is loath to lose me.

10. (III)

O might those sighs and tears that I have spent return
To my breast and eyes
So I might in my holy discontent
Mourn fruitfully, since I have mourned in vain.
In my idolatry what showers of rain
Did my eyes waste! By what griefs my heart was torn!
Such suffering was my sin; now I repent.
Because I did suffer I must now suffer pain.
The thirsty drunkard and night-scouting thief,
The itchy leper and the proud self
Remember past joys, for relief of coming ills.
I am allowed no ease,
For passionate grief has been the cause and effect, my
punishment and my sin.

11. (IV)

    Oh, my impure soul, now you are summoned

    By sickness, which is death's herald and advocate.

    You are like a pilgrim who has committed treason in a foreign
        country,

    And you dare not return to the country from which you've fled.

    Or like a thief, that until death's doom be read,

    Wishes himself delivered from prison;

    But when called by death, he wishes he were still in prison.

    If you repent, though, you will not lack grace.

    But who will give you that grace to begin?

    Make yourself black with holy mourning,

    Make yourself as red with blushing as you are with sin.

    Wash yourself in Christ's blood. For his blood has this power:

    Being red, his blood dyes red souls to white.

12. (V)

    I am a little world made cunningly

    Of elements and an angelic sprite,

    But black sin has betrayed to endless night

    Both parts of my world, and both parts must die.

    You, who have found new spheres and lands beyond that
        heaven most high,

    Pour new seas in my eyes, so I might drown my world with
        earnest weeping.

    If it cannot be drowned, wash it;

    But it must be burned, for the fires of lust and envy have
        already burned it and made it fouler.

    Let the flames burn me, O Lord, with your fiery zeal, which
        heals as it consumes.

13. (VI)

This is my play's last scene; this is my pilgrimage's last mile.
My race, idly but quickly run, has this last pace,
Gluttonous death will instantly separate
My body and soul, and I shall sleep a space.
But my eternal soul will see God's face
Whose fear already shakes every joint.
Then, as my soul takes flight to heaven, her first seat,
My body will remain on the earth.
Fall my sins to where you are bred and would press me to hell.
With my evil thus removed, impute me righteous,
For thus I leave the world, the flesh, and the devil.

14. (VII)

Angels, blow your trumpets at the earth's imagined corners.
Arise from death, you numberless souls, and go to your
    scattered bodies,
All whom the flood drowned and the fire will overthrow,
All whom war, death, age, fevers, tyrannies, despair, law, and
    chance have slain,
And you, whose eyes will behold God and never taste death's
    woe.
But let them sleep, Lord, and me mourn a space,
For, if my sins abound above all these,
It is too late for me to ask for the abundance of your grace
    when we are with you.
Teach me how to repent here on this lowly ground,
For that is as good as if you had sealed my pardon with your
    blood.

15. (VIII)

If faithful souls are glorified like the angels
Then my father's soul sees and adds to this happiness
So that I stride over hell's wide mouth.
But if our minds be descried to these souls by circumstances
    and signs apparent in us,
How can they try my mind's pure truth?
They see idolatrous lovers weep and mourn and vile
    blasphemous magicians call on Jesus
And Pharisaical dissemblers feign devotion.
Turn, o pensive soul, to God, for he knows best
Your true grief, for he put it in your heart.

16. (IX)

If poisonous minerals, and that tree
Whose fruit caused death to otherwise immortal creatures;
If lecherous goats and envious serpents cannot be damned,
    why should I be damned?
Why should my intent or reason, born in me,
Make sins, otherwise equal, more heinous in me?
And mercy being easy and glorious to God,
Why does he threaten me with his stern wrath?
Who am I that I dare dispute with you, O God?
Of your only worthy blood and my tears make a heavenly
Lethean flood,
And drown in it my sin's black memory.
That you remember our sins some claim as a debt,
I think it is mercy, if you will forget.

17. (X)

Death be not proud, though some have called you
Mighty and dreadful, for you are not so,
For those you think you overthrow
Do not die, poor death, nor can you yet kill me.

From rest and sleep, which are nothing but imitations of you,
Much pleasure, then from you, much more must flow,
And soon our best people go with you,
Rest of their bones and soul's delivery.
You are slave to fate, chance, kings, and desperate men,
And dwell with poison, war, and sickness,
Poppies or charms make us sleep as well
And better than your stroke; Why do you swell up with pride
    then?
One short sleep past, we wake eternally,
And death shall be no more; death, you shall die.

18. (XI)

Spit in my face, you Jews, and pierce my side,
Scoff, scourge, and crucify me,
For I have sinned and sinned, and only he
Who could not sin, has died:
But my sins, which surpass the Jews' impiety, cannot be
    satisfied by my death.
They killed once an inglorious man, but I
Crucify him daily, being now glorified.
Let me then admire his strange love:
Kings pardon, but he bore our punishment.
Jacob came clothed in vile harsh attire
To supplant with gainful intent.
God clothed himself in vile human flesh, so that
He might be weak enough to suffer woe.

19. (XII)

Why are we waited upon by all creatures?
Why do the prodigal elements supply
Life and food to me, since they are more pure than I,
Simple, and farther from corruption?
Why does the ignorant horse endure subjection?

Why do the bull and boar so sillily disguise weakness
And die at the hand of one person, whose whole race you
    might swallow and feed upon?
You animals have not sinned, nor need be afraid.
Wonder at a greater wonder, for to us
Created nature subdues these things,
But their Creator, whom neither sin nor nature tied,
For his creatures, his foes, and us has died.

20. (XIII)

What if this present were the world's last night?
Mark in my heart, O soul, where you dwell,
The picture of Christ crucified, and tell
Whether that face can scare you,
Tears in his eyes quench the amazing light,
Blood fills his frowns, that from his pierced head fell,
And can that tongue, that prayed forgiveness for his enemies'
    fierce spite, settle you into hell?
No, but as in my idolatry
I said to all my profane mistresses,
Beauty, of pity, foulness is a sign of rigor; so I say to you
Horrid shapes are assigned to wicked spirits,
This beauteous form assures a piteous mind.

21. (XIV)

Batter my heart, three-personed God; for, you
As yet but knock, breathe, shine, and seek to mend;
So that I may rise and stand, throw me down and use
Your force to break, blow, burn, and make me new.
I, like a usurped town, to another due,
Labor to admit you, but to no end.
Reason, your viceroy in me, should defend me
But is captive and proves weak or untrue.
Yet I would love you dearly, and would be loved willingly,
Except I am engaged to your enemy.

Divorce me, untie, or break that knot again,
Take me to you, imprison me, for I,
Unless you do imprison me, shall never be free,
Nor will I be chaste, unless you ravish me.

22. (XV)

Will you love God as he loves you?
Then, my soul, digest this wholesome meditation.
How God the Spirit, waited on by angels in heaven,
Makes his temple in your breast.
The Father having engendered a most blessed Son,
And still creating,
Deigned to adopt you,
Co-heir to his glory and Sabbath's endless rest.
As a robbed person searches for and finds his stolen goods
Must lose them or buy them again:
The Son of glory came down, and was slain
To unbind us whom he made and whom Satan had stolen.
It was much that man was in God's image,
But it was even more that God should be made like man.

23. (XVI)

Father, your Son gives me part of his double interest
    in Your kingdom,
He keeps his inheritance in the knotty Trinity,
And gives me his death's conquest.
This Lamb, whose death has blessed this world with life,
Slain from the beginning of the world,
Has made two wills, which with the legacy
Of his and your kingdom, do your sons invest.
Yet such are your laws that men still argue
Whether a man can fulfill them.
None can fulfill them, but your all-healing grace and Spirit
Revive again what the law and the letter kill.

Your law's abridgement, and your last command
Is to love; let that last will stand!

24. (XVII)

Since she whom I loved has paid her last debt
To Nature, and to hers and my good is dead,
And her Soul was carried away early into heaven,
My mind is set entirely on heavenly things.
Admiring her, my mind was whetted
To seek you, God; so streams do show their head
But though I have found you, and you have fed my thirst,
A holy thirsty dropsy melts me yet.
Why should I beg for more Love; when as you
Woo my soul for hers, offering all yours
And are not afraid that I might give
My Love to Saints and Angels,
But in your tender jealousy do doubt
Least the World, Flesh, and the Devil put you out.

25. (XVIII)

Show me, dear Christ, your spouse, so bright and clear.
Is it She, that on the other shore
Goes richly painted? Or was it she, so richly clothed, that tore
Laments in Germany and here?
Does she sleep a thousand years and then peep up one year?
Is she herself both truth and error? Now new, now worn out?
Does she, and did she, and will she evermore
Appear on one, or seven, or no hill?
Does she dwell with us, or like adventuring knights
Do we labor to find her and then make Love?
Kind husband, betray your spouse to our sights,
And let my amorous soul court your mild Dove,
For she is most true, and pleasing to you,
When she is embraced and open to most men.

26. (XIX)

Oh, to vex me, contraries have met in one:
Inconstancy unnaturally has engendered
A constant habit, so that when I do not want to
I change in vows and devotion.
As humorous is my contrition
As my profane Love, and as soon forgot:
As riddlingly distempered, cold and hot,
As praying, as mute; as infinite, as none.
I dared not view heaven yesterday, and today
I court God in prayers and flattering speeches:
Tomorrow I quake with true fear of his rod.
So my devout fits come and go away
Like a fantastic fever, except that here
Those are my best days, when I shake with fear.

The Cross

Since Christ embraced the Cross itself, do I dare
Deny his image, which is the image of his Cross?
Would I have profited by the sacrifice,
Daring to despise the chosen Altar?
It bore all other sins, but is it fitting
That it should bear the sin of scorning it?
Who would avert his eye from the picture,
How would he fly from his pains, who there did die?
This Cross shall not withdraw neither from me, nor any
Pulpit, nor any misgrounded law,
Nor any scandal taken.
It will not, for it cannot; the loss
Of this Cross would be to me another Cross to bear.
Better were worse, for no affliction,
No Cross is so extreme as to have no Cross.

Who can blot out the Cross, which the instrument
Of God poured on me in the sacrament of baptism?
Who can deny me power and liberty
To stretch my arms and to be my own Cross?
Swim, and at every stroke, you form your own Cross;
The Mast and yard are united where the seas toss;
Look down and you see Crosses in small things;
Look up and you see birds raised on crossed wings,
All the Globe's frame and spheres are nothing else
But Meridians crossing Parallels.
Material Crosses are good medicine,
But spiritual Crosses have chief dignity.
These serve as extracted chemic medicine,
And cure much better and preserve.
Then you are your own medicine, or need none,
When stilled, or purged, by tribulation.
For when that Cross sticks to you willingly,
Then you are to yourself a crucifix.
As perchance, carvers do not make faces,
But that away, which hid them there, do take:
So, let Crosses take what Christ hid in you,
And be his image, or not his, but he.
But, as often as alchemists prove to be coiners,
So may a self-despising get self-love.
And then as the worst satiety of the best meats is,
So does pride issue from humility.
For it is no child but a monster; therefore cross
Your joy in crosses, otherwise it is a double loss,
And cross your senses, otherwise both you and they
Must perish soon, and bow to destruction.
For if the eye seeks good objects, and will take
No cross from bad, we cannot escape a snake.
So with harsh, hard, sour, stinking cross the rest,

Make them indifferent; call nothing best.
But most the eye needs crossing, that can roam,
And move; to the others the objects must come home,
And cross your heart: for it in man alone
Points downwards and palpitates.
Cross those dejections, when it downward tends,
And when it to forbidden heights pretends.
And as the brain through bony walls does divulge
By sutures, that a cross's form presents,
When your brain works, before you utter it,
Cross and correct concupiscence of wit.
Covet Crosses, let none fall.
Cross no one else, but cross yourself in all.
Then does the Cross of Christ work fruitfully
Within our hearts, when we love harmlessly
That Cross's pictures, and with more care
That Cross's children, which are our Crosses.

A Hymn to Christ

In whatever ragged ship I embark,
That ship will be an emblem of your ark;
Whatever sea swallows me, that flood
Shall be to me an emblem of your blood;
Though with clouds of anger you disguise your face,
Even through that mask I know those eyes,
   Which, even though they sometimes turn away,
     They never will despise.
I sacrifice this Island to you
And all I have loved there, and all who love me;
When I have put the seas between them and me,
Put your sea between my sins and me.

As a tree's sap seeks the roots in winter,
In winter now I go,
  Where no one but you, the eternal root of true love,
    I may know.
Neither you nor your religion controls
The amorousness of the soul,
But you would have that love yourself
As you are jealous, Lord, so I am jealous now,
You love not, until from loving more, you free my soul,
Whoever gives, takes liberty:
  If you do not care whom I love,
    You do not love me.
Seal then this bill of divorce from everyone,
On whom fell those fainter beams of love;
Join to yourself those loves that in youth are scattered
On fame, wit, hopes.
Churches that have least light are best for prayer:
To see God only I go out of sight
  And to escape stormy days, I choose
    An everlasting night.

Hymn to God My God, In My Sickness

Since I am coming to that holy room,
  Where, with your choir of saints for evermore,
I shall be made your music; as I come
  I tune the instrument here at the door,
  And what must I do then, think now before.
While my physicians by their love are grown
  Cosmographers, and I am their map, who lies
Flat on this bed, that by them may be shown
  That this is my south-west discovery
  Through the straits of fever to die.

I rejoice that in these straits I see my west;
    For, though their currents yield return to no one,
What shall my west hurt me? As west and east
      In all flat maps (and I am one) are one,
      So death is one with the resurrection.
Is the Pacific Sea my home? Or are
      The eastern riches? Is Jerusalem
Anyan, and Magellan, and Gibraltar,
      All straits are ways to them
      Whether Japhet, Ham, or Shem dwelt there.
We think that Paradise and Calvary,
    Christ's Cross, and Adam's tree, stood in one place;
Look Lord, and find both Adams met in me;
      As the first Adam's sweat surrounds my face,
      May the last Adam's blood my soul embrace.
So, wrapped in his purple the Lord received me,
    By these thorns give me his other crown;
And as to others' souls I preached your word,
      Be this my text, my sermon to myself,
      So he may raise up the Lord throws down.

A Hymn to God the Father

I
Will you forgive that sin where I began,
    Which is my sin, though it was done before me?
Will you forgive those sins through which I run,
      And do them still, even though I them deplore?
        When you have finished, you have not finished,
          For I have more.

II

Will you forgive that sin by which I have won
    Others to sin and made sin their door?
Will you forgive that sin which I did shun
     A year or two, but which I wallowed in for twenty more?
       When you have finished, you have not finished,
         For I have more.

III

I have a sin of fear that when I have spun
    My last thread, I will perish on the shore;
     Swear that at my death your Sun
Will shine as it now shines, and thus,
     Having done that, you have finished,
      I fear no more.

Upon the Annunciation and Passion Falling on one Day

Abstain today frail body; today
My soul eats twice, Christ here and away.
She sees him as a human and so much like God,
That their natures are like a circle
Whose beginning and end concur; this doubtful day
Of feast or fast, Christ came, and went away.
Twice at once, she sees him who is all as nothing;
She sees a cedar plant itself and then fall,
Her Maker put to making, and the head
Of life, at once, not yet alive, and dead;
She sees at once the virgin mother
Privately at home and publicly at Golgotha.
She is seen as sad and joyous at once, and seen
At almost fifty, and when she's scarcely fifteen.
A Son is promised to her, and he is gone,

Gabriel gives Christ to her, and he gives her to John;
Not fully a mother, she is in grief,
At once receiver and legacy;
All this and everything between this day has shown,
The abridgment of Christ's story, which makes a unity
Of the angel's blessing and the dying words of Christ.
How well the Church, God's court of faculties
Deals in only sometimes and very seldom joining these;
As by the fixed pole star we never do
Direct our course, but the nearest star to it,
Shows us where the other one is, and the pole star of which
    we say
It never does stray.
So we know God by his Church because it is nearest to him,
And we stand firm if we follow her direction;
His Spirit, as his fiery pillar does
Lead, and his Church, as a cloud; to one end both:
This Church, by letting these days join, has shown
Death and conception are one in humankind:
Or in him was the same humility,
That he would choose to take the form of a man:
Or because of the creation he has made, as God,
With the last judgment, all one eternal period,
His imitating spouse would join in one
Humanity's extremes: he will come, he is gone;
Or, as though one drop of blood that fell,
Would have been enough, he shed it all;
So though the least of his pains, deeds, or words,
Would busy a life, she all this day affords;
This treasure, then, in gross, my soul unplay,
And in my life retell it every day.

Good Friday, 1613. Riding Westward.

Let man's soul be a sphere, and then, in this,
The intelligence that moves, devotion is,
And as the other spheres, by being grown
Subject to foreign motions, lose their own,
And being by others hurried every day,
Scarce in a year their natural form obey:
Pleasure or business, so, our souls admit
For their first mover, and are whirled by it.
Hence is it that I am carried toward the West
This day, when my soul's form bends toward the East.
There I should see a Sun, by rising set,
And by that setting endless days beget;
Unless Christ on this Cross did rise and fall,
Sin would have eternally benighted all.
Yet dare I almost be glad I do not see
That spectacle of too much weight for me.
Who sees God's face, that is in itself life, must die;
What a death were it then to see God die?
It made his own Lieutenant Nature shrink,
It made his own footstool crack and the Sun wink.
Could I behold those hands which span the Poles,
And turn all spheres at once, pierced with those holes?
Could I behold that endless height which is
Zenith to us and our Antipodes,
Humbled below us? Or that blood which is
The seat of all our Souls, if not of his,
Made dirt of dust, or that flesh which was worn
By God for his apparel, ragged and torn?
If on these things I do not look, dare I
Upon this miserable mother cast my eye,
Who was God's partner here, and furnished thus
Half of that sacrifice which ransomed us?

Though these things, as I ride, be far from mine eye,
They are present yet to my memory,
For that looks toward them; and you look oft toward me,
O Savior, as you hang upon the tree;
I turn my back to you, only to receive
Corrections, till your mercies bid me leave.
I think me worth your anger, punish me,
Burn off my rusts, and my deformity,
Restore your Image, so much, by your grace,
That you may know me, and I'll turn my face.

The Litany

I   *The Father*
Father of heaven, and he, by whom
It, and us for it, and all else, for us
You made and govern forever, come
And recreate me, who have been damned:
    My heart is by dejection, clay,
    And by self-murder, red.
From this red earth, O Father, purge
All corrupt stains, so that newly fashioned
I may rise up from death before I am dead.

II.   *The Son*
O Son of God, who, seeing two things,
Sin and death, which were never made,
By bearing one, tried by the stings
The other invaded your heritage.
    Be nailed to my heart,
    And crucified again,
Do not part from it, though it would part from you,
But by applying your pain let
My heart be drowned in your blood, and extinguished in your
    passion.

III. *The Holy Spirit*
    O Holy Spirit, whose temple I
    Am, but of mud walls and condensed dust,
    Sacrilegiously
    Half-wasted with youth's fires of pride and lust,
        I must be weather-beaten with new storms.
        Double in my heart your flame,
    Which let devout sad tears intensify, and let
    (Though this flesh suffer injury)
    Fire, sacrifice, priest, altar be the same.

IV. *The Trinity*
    O Blessed glorious Trinity,
    Bones to philosophy, but milk to faith,
    Which as wise serpents
    Are slippery and tangled
        As you are at once separate and inseparable
        And as you are power, love, and knowledge,
    Give me such an identity,
    And let these be my elements,
    Of power, to love, to know, you unnumbered three.

V. *The Virgin Mary*
    For that fair blessed mother-maid,
    Whose flesh redeemed us; that she-angel
    That unlocked Paradise and made
    One claim for innocence and dispossessed sin,
        Whose womb was a strange heaven, for there
        God clothed himself and grew,
    Our zealous thanks we pour out to you. As her deeds were
    Our helps, so are her prayers; nor can she sue
    In vain, who has such titles unto you.

VI. *The Angels*
    Since this life is our immaturity,
    And your angels are our guardians,
    Native to heaven's fair palaces
    Where we will become natural citizens,
    As the earth conceiving by the sun,
    Yields fair diversity,
    Yet never knows which course that light runs,
    So teach me so my actions may be
    Worthy in their sight, though they are blind in the ways they see.

VII. *The Patriarchs*
    Let your Patriarchs' desire
    (Those great grandfathers of your Church, which saw
    More in the cloud than we in the fire,
    Whom Nature taught more than we learned from grace and law,
        And now in heaven still pray that we
        May use our new helps in the right way)
    Be satisfied and be fruit in me;
    Do not let my mind be blinder because of more light
    Nor faith, by adding reason, lose her sight.

VIII. *The Prophets*
    Your eagle-eyed prophets too,
    That were your Church's organs and declared
    That harmony that took two testaments and made
    One law, united them but did not alter or confuse them;
        Those heavenly poets did see
        Your will and express it
    In rhythmic feet; pray for me,
    That because of them I do not excuse my excess
    In seeking secrets or in my poeticness.

IX. *The Apostles*
> Your illustrious zodiac
> Of twelve apostles that encircles all this
> (Do not take their light away from people);
>> Through their prayers you have let me know
>> That their books are divine.
> May they still pray and be heard, so that I go
> The old broad way in applying the Scripture's message,
> Do not let my words replace the words of your word.

X. *The Martyrs*
> Since you so desired
> And did want to die long before you could,
> And long since you could no more die
> In your scattered mystic body
>> In Abel died, and ever since
>> In yours, let their blood come
> To ask for us a discreet patience
> In waiting for death, or of a worse life. For to some
> Not to be martyrs is a martyrdom.

XI. *The Confessors*
> With you there triumph
> A virgin squadron of pure confessors,
> Whose bloods were engaged but never married;
> Though presented, you were not taken by the violators:
>> They know and pray that we may know
>> In every Christian
> Hourly tempestuous persecutions grow,
> Temptations martyr us alive; a person
> Is to himself a Diocletian.

XII. *The Virgins*
    The cold white snowy nunnery,
    That, as your mother, their high abbess, sent
    Their bodies back again to you,
    Just as you had lent them, clean and innocent,
        Though they have not obtained you
        I and your Church
    Should keep, like they, our first righteousness;
    Divorce sin in us, or bid it die,
    And call pure widowhood virginity.

XIII. *The Doctors*
    Your sacred academy above
    Of Theologians whose studies have opened and taught
    Both books of life to us (for love
    To know your Scriptures tells us, we are fashioned
        In your other book) pray for us there
        That what they have misinterpreted
    That we may not adhere to that;
    Their zeal may be our sin. Lord, let us run
    A middle way, and call the theologians the stars but not the sun.

XIV.
    While this universal choir,
    That Church in triumph, it is warfare here,
    Warmed with all one-partaking fire
    Of love, that none be lost, it cost you dearly,
        Prays ceaselessly and you listen
        Since to be gracious
    Our task is tripled: to pray, bear, and do)
    Hear this prayer, Lord; O Lord, deliver us
    From trusting in those prayers though poured out thus.

XV.

>Good Lord, deliver us
From being anxious or secure,
Dead clods of sadness, or light squibs of humor,
From thinking that great courts confine
All happiness, or that this earth
>>Is only our prison framed
>>Or that you are jealous
Of them whom you love, or that they are prevented
From reaching this world's sweet, who seek you
With all their might.

XVI.

>Lord, deliver us
From needing danger to be good,
From owing you yesterday's tears today,
From trusting so much to your blood,
That in that hope we twist our soul away
>>From bribing you with alms to excuse
>>Some more burdensome sin,
From frivolously espousing new religious beliefs,
From thinking us all soul, thus neglecting
Our mutual duties.

XVII.

>Deliver us
From tempting Satan to tempt us
By our trickery or by weak company
From measuring sin by vice, no virtue,
Neglecting to choke sin's child, vanity,
>>From indiscreet humility,
>>Which might be scandalous,
And cast reproach on Christianity,
From being spies or vulnerable to spies,
From thirst or scorn of fame.

XVIII.

Deliver us for your descent
Into the Virgin, whose womb was a place
Of middle kind; and you, being sent
To us who were ungracious, stayed in her full of grace
And through your poor birth, where you first
Glorified poverty,
And yet soon after riches did allow,
By accepting Kings' gifts in the Epiphany,
Deliver and make us to both ways free.

XIX.

Through that bitter agony
Which is still the agony of pious wits,
Disputing what distorted you
And interrupted evenness, with fits,
And through your free confession
Though they were then
Made blind, so that from them you might have gone,
Good Lord deliver us, and teach us when
We may not and when we may blind unjust men.

XX.

Through submitting all to blows,
Your face, your clothes to spoil, your fame to scorn,
All ways that rage or justice know,
And by which you could show that you were born
Through your gallant humbleness
Which you showed in death,
Dying before your soul they could kill,
Deliver us from death, by dying so
To this world, before this world bids us to go.

XXI.

When senses, which are your soldiers,
We arm against you, and they fight for sin;
When poverty, sent but to tame, does battle
And work despair a breach to enter in,
　　When plenty, God's image and seal
　　Makes us idolatrous
And we love it, not him whom it should reveal,
When we are moved to seem religious
Only to vent our wits, Lord, deliver us.

XXII.

In churches when the infirmity
Of the speaker diminishes the Word,
When magistrates do not correctly apply
To us, as we judge it, secular or spiritual punishment
　　When plague, your angel, reigns
　　Or wars your champions win,
When heresy, your second flood, gains;
In the hour of death, the eve of last judgment day,
Deliver us from the sinister way.

XXIII.

Hear us, O Lord; to you
A sinner is more music when he prays
Than are the spheres or the angels' praises
In their alleluias.
　　Hear us, for until you hear us, Lord,
　　We do not know what to say.
Your hearing our sighs, tears, thoughts, gives voice and word.
You who heard Satan in Job's sickest day,
Hear yourself now, for you are in us as we pray.

XXIV.

    That we may change to evenness
    This intermittent feverish piety
    That snatching cramps of wickedness
    And apoplexies of easy sin may die.
        That music of your promises,
        Not threats in thunder, may
    Awaken us to our just offices
    What in your book you or creatures say
    That we may hear, Lord, hear us when we pray.

XXV.

    So that we may cure our ears' sickness
    And straighten those labyrinths
    That by listening we do not encourage
    Our praise or invite the dispraise of others.
        So that we do not slip
        And senselessly decline
    From hearing bold wits' jest at kings' excess
    To admit the likeness of majesty divine
    So that we may close our ears, Lord, open yours.

XXVI.

    That living law, the magistrate,
    Which to give us health does
    Often aggravate our vices,
    The preacher's taxing sin, before its growth,
        That Satan, and poisonous men
        Which will, if we starve, dine,
    When they do most accuse us, may you see
    Us hear them for our own good; you refuse to hear them and
    Open our ears, Lord, close yours.

XXVII.

> That learning, your ambassador,
> From your allegiance we never tempt,
> That beauty, paradise's flower
> For medicine made, from poison exempt,
> > That wit, born apt, high good to do,
> > By dwelling lazily
> On Nature's nothing, be not nothing too,
> That our affections will not kill us, nor die,
> Hear us, weak echoes, Source of prayer.

XXVIII.

> Son of God, hear us, and since you,
> By taking our blood, owe it to us again,
> Gain to yourself or to us yield;
> And do not let both of us and yourself be slain;
> > O Lamb of God, which took our sin
> > Which could not stick to you,
> Do not let it return to us again
> But patient and doctor being free,
> As sin is nothing, let it nowhere be.

CHAPTER II
Sermons

1. *The Preacher*
   In the great anthill of the whole world, I am an ant. I have my part in the creation; I am a creature. In the great field of clay, of red earth that humanity was made of, I am a clod. I am a man and am part of humanity. Humanity was worse than destroyed again when Satan, disguised as a serpent, came and destroyed all humankind. The gracious promise of a Messiah to redeem all humanity was shed and spread out for all. I had my drop of that dew of heaven, my spark of that fire of heaven, in the universal promise that had been given to me. But the Jews, the seed of Abraham, assimilated this promise in a particular covenant. However, I have my portion there, for all who profess Christ belong to the seed of Abraham through spiritual grafting. I am one of those. But, then, some of those who profess Jesus Christ still grovel in the superstitions they had fallen into, and some are raised out of these superstitions by God's grace. I am one of them. God has provided me with my station, which is in that Church now departed from Babylon.

2. *When I Consider*
   Amorous soul, ambitious soul, covetous soul, voluptuous soul, what would you desire in heaven? What does your holy amorousness, your holy covetousness, your holy ambition, and your holy voluptuousness focus your desire upon? Call it what you will; think it what you can; think it is something that you

cannot think; and all this you will have, if you have any Resurrection unto life. Yet there is a Better Resurrection. When I consider what I was in my parent's loins (a substance unworthy of a word, unworthy of a thought); when I consider what I am now (a volume of diseases bound up together, a dry cinder, an aged child, a gray-headed infant, and but the ghost of my own youth); when I consider what I will be at last, by the hand of death, in my grave (for a while all worms, and after a while, sordid, senseless, nameless dust); when I consider the past, present, and future state of this body in this world, I can express the worst that can happen to it in nature as well as the worst that misfortune and other people can inflict upon it. But I am unable to express the least degree of glory that God has prepared for this body in heaven.

3. *Imperfect Prayers*

It is sad to consider the many weaknesses of even the strongest devotions in times of prayer. I throw myself down in my chamber and invite God and his angels there. When they are there, I neglect them when I hear the noise of a rattling coach or the squeaking of a door. I pray as if I were talking to God, with my eyes lifted up and my knees bowed down. But if God or his angels asked me when I last thought about God during that same prayer, I could not tell them. Sometimes I find that I have forgotten what I am doing, but just when I forgot, I cannot tell. A memory of yesterday's pleasures, a fear of tomorrow's dangers, a piece of straw under my knee, a noise in my ear, a light in my eye, anything takes my attention away from my prayer. There is nothing in spiritual things that is perfect in this world.

4. *Powers and Principalities*

I pass my time sociably and merrily in cheerful conversation, in music, in feasting, in comedies, in wantonness. All the time I am engaging in such activities I never hear of any power or principality, and my conscience sees no enemy in these activities. Then, when I am alone with God at midnight, some beam of his grace shines out upon me, and I see by that light the Prince of darkness. Then I discover I have been the slave of these powers and principalities, when I did not think about them. Well, I see them and I try to dispossess myself of them through the most powerful exorcism I know, hearty and earnest prayer to God. I fix my thoughts strongly upon him, and before I have perfected one prayer, a power and principality has got into me again. The spirit of slumber closes my eyes, and I pray drowsily. The spirit of deviation and vain repetition enters, and I pray circularly, returning over and over to what I have already said, and I do not know I'm doing this. I pray and do not know of what spirit I am, not knowing or considering what my purpose is in praying. Through this door the seducing spirit enters, and I pray not only negligently, but also erroneously and dangerously, for such things are not conducive to God's glory or my true happiness. The spirit of fornication, that is, some remembrance of the wantonness of my youth, some misinterpretation of a word in prayer that may have a perverted meaning, enters my prayer. Some unclean spirit, some power or principality, has depraved my prayer and slackened my zeal.

5. *Infecting God*

Chrysostom says that every person is *Spontaneous Satan*, a Satan to himself, for as Satan is a Tempter, every person can tempt himself. So I will be *Spontaneous Satan*, as Satan is an accuser and adversary, I will accuse myself. I often consider Peter's passionate humiliation: "He fell at Jesus' knees, saying,

'Depart from me, for I am a sinful man, O Lord.'" And I am ready to say all this and more. Depart from me, O Lord, for I am sinful enough to infect you. Just as I persecute your children, I infect you in your ordinances. Depart, in withdrawing your word from me, for I am corrupt enough to make even your saving gospel the savor of death. Depart, in withholding your Sacrament, for I am leprous enough to taint your flesh, to make the balm of your blood poison to my soul. Depart, in withholding the protection of your angels from me, for I am vicious enough to imprint corruption and rebellion into their nature. If I am too foul for God Himself to come near me, for His laws to work upon me, then I am not fit to be a companion for myself. I must not be alone with myself, for I am as likely to take as to give infection. I am a reciprocal plague, passively and actively contagious. I breathe corruption, and I breathe it upon my self. I am the Babylon that I must leave, or I will die.

6.   *Forgiveness of Sins*

As the Spirit of God moves upon the face of the waters, the Spirit of life moves upon the danger of death. Consider God's love and diligence. He devises means so that those banished by sin and death are not expelled from him. When I was young, I sinned heartily; God used a debilitating sickness to reclaim me. I relapsed after my recovery, and God reclaimed me by means of an irrecoverable consumption. My consumption grew so heavy upon me that I was indifferent even to God's mercy; so God provided me with the comfort of his minister, the angel of his Church, and the body and blood of Christ Jesus, the angel of great counsel. Yet God lets his correction follow one until death. I die of that sickness, but God devises a means so that I, even though banished into the grave, will not be expelled from him, a glorious Resurrection.

7. *Forgive My Sins*

Forgive me, O Lord, the sins of my youth, my present sins, the sin my Parents cast upon me, and the sin I cast upon my children by my bad example. Forgive me of those sins that all the world witnesses me perform as well as those sins I have hidden so well from the world that I have also hidden them from myself. Forgive me of my sins of uncharitable hate and impure love, sins against You, against Your Power, Almighty Father, against Your Wisdom, O glorious Son, against your Goodness, O blessed Spirit of God. Forgive me the sins against my own soul and against my own body, which I have loved better than my soul. Forgive me, O Lord, with the grace of your Christ and my Jesus, your Anointed one and my Savior. Say to me, "Blessed are they whose sins are forgiven." Let me be so blessed, and I will envy no person's blessedness. Say to my sad soul, "Be of good comfort, your sins are forgiven," and I will not trouble you with prayers asking you to reverse any decree that accuses me before you saw me as a sinner.

8. *Donne and the Worms*

My soul would like to ask one of the worms that my dead body will produce, "Will you change with me?" That worm would say, "No, for you are likely to live in eternal torment. As for me, I will not change when I die. Indeed, would the Devil himself change places with a damned soul? I cannot tell."

9. *Preaching Consolation*

Who but I can imagine the sweetness of the Spirit of God's morning greeting, "Go forth today and preach consolation, peace, and mercy. Spare my people whom I have redeemed with my precious blood, and do not be angry with them forever. Do not wound them or overwhelm them with the bitterness, the heaviness, the sharpness and consternation of my judgments." When David proposes to sing of mercy and judgment (Ps. 101:1), he sings of mercy first. The good angels, the ministerial angels of the Church, are God's proper instruments for conveying mercy, peace, and consolation.

10. *The Beauty of the Soul*

Saint Paul was mad for love. He took into his contemplation, as we should also, the beauty of a Christian soul. Through the ragged clothes of this life's afflictions, the scars, wounds, paleness, and corruption, we look upon the soul itself and see its incorruptible beauty. We can see the white and red, which Christ's innocence and blood have given it, and we are mad for love of this soul. We are ready to be persecuted or humiliated so we may stand at the soul's door and pray that she would be reconciled to God.

11. *The Bellman*

The person that will die with Christ on Good Friday hears his own death knoll all through Lent. Whoever would partake of Christ's passion must imitate Christ's discipline of prayer and fasting. Is there anyone who hears death's bell toll for another person who does not kneel down and pray for the dying person? Then, when his love breathes out upon another, does he not also reflect upon himself and prepare himself as if he were dying? We begin to hear Christ's bell toll now. Isn't our bell in that chime? We must be in Christ's grave before we come to his resurrection, and we must be in his deathbed before we are in his grave. We must fast and pray, as he did, before we can say, with Christ, "Into your hands, Lord, I commend my Spirit." Do not say to yourselves, "We will have enough preparation and warnings and sermons before we die." You are not sure you will have more or that those words will affect you in any way. If you hear cheerful street music on winter mornings, remember that a sad and mournful bellman awakened you a few hours earlier. So, for all the blessed music that the servants of God present to you in this place, remember that a poor bellman awakened you and prepared you for their music.

12. *Favorite Scriptures*

Almost everyone has an appetite, and his taste is disposed to some kinds of food rather than others. He knows what dish he would choose for his first and second course. We have the same disposition in our spiritual diet. A person may have a particular love for one or another book of Scripture. I acknowledge that my spiritual appetite leads me to the Psalms of David as my first course and the Epistles of Saint Paul as my second course. My meditations for my preaching return most often to these two. For, as a host offers to his guests the food he loves best, so I often present to God's people meditations drawn from those two Scriptures. If a person is asked why he loves one food better than another, where all are equally good (as the books of Scripture are), he will at least try to find a good example. For my diet, I have Saint Augustine's exclamation that he loved the Book of Psalms and Saint Chrysostom's cry that he loved Saint Paul's Epistles with particular devotion. Another reason I love these two Scriptures is that they are written in such forms, letters and poems, that I am most accustomed to. God gives us instructions in cheerful forms, not in a sour, sullen, angry, and unacceptable way. Therefore, God's will is delivered in Psalms, so we may have his will cheerfully and certainly. Let us, then, not pray or preach slackly, unadvisedly, or without diligence. Let all our speech to God be weighed and measured carefully, and let us be content to pray to God in those forms that the Church has recommended for us.

13. *The Psalms*

The Psalms are the manna of the Church. Just as manna tasted to each person like the food that the person liked best, so the Psalms instruct and satisfy every person in every occasion. David was not only a clear prophet of Christ himself, but a prophet of every particular Christian. The entire book of Psalms is a fragrant oil, an ointment that soothes all sorts of sores, and a balm that heals all wounds. There are certain universal and catholic Psalms that apply to all occasions.

14. *Sanctified Passions*

The prophets and other secretaries of the Holy Spirit retain some air of their former professions in their writings. Those who had once been fishermen, shepherds, and herdsmen are forever inserting phrases, allusions, and other metaphors from their former professions into their writings. The soul that has been transported from worldly pleasure, when it is entirely turned upon God, finds God a fit subject on which to exercise the same affection in pious and religious terms.

A covetous person, now truly converted to God, will exercise a spiritual covetousness. This person will desire to have all of God, and he will covet security and the seal and the assurance of the Holy Spirit. He wants to have his good life and his conversation witnessed throughout the world. He applies his faith so he may have all that God has promised, all Christ has purchased, all the Holy Spirit holds in its stewardship. A covetous person converted will be a spiritually covetous person.

A sensual person who turns to God will find him delicious and plentiful enough to feed his soul with marrow and fatness. An angry and passionate person will find enough zeal in the house of God to consume him.

God justly employs all passions that are common to all people as well as those to which particular people have been addicted, for we cannot go too far in using those passions against God. Accordingly, Saint Paul, who had been a violent persecutor of Christians, after his conversion to Christianity mentions his own suffering more than any of the other Apostles. Also, Solomon, who loved women excessively, when he invested his forms and habits with his spiritual outlook, began to apply these loving approaches to God.

15. *The Indifference of Nature*

A fountain erupts in the wilderness, but that fountain does not care whether people drink from it or not. A fresh wind blows upon the sea, but the wind does not care whether sailors hoist their sails or not. A rose blossoms in your garden, but it does not care whether you come to smell it or not.

16. *Afflictions*

All our life is a continual burden, but we must not groan under this burden. As in our childhood, we suffer, but we are whipped if we cry over our ills. This sad consideration becomes even sadder when we realize that the best people have the most suffering laid upon them. When God says of Job, "I have found an upright man who fears God and avoids evil," we read that God authorizes Satan to kill Job's cattle, servants, and children, and to afflict Job with horrible diseases. When we read that God has found a "man according to his own heart," we read that his sons rape his daughters, then murder one another, then rebel against their father. When we read that God testifies to Christ at his baptism, "This is my beloved Son in whom I am well pleased," we soon read that the Son is "led out by the Spirit to be tempted by the Devil."

But there is "an exceeding weight of eternal glory" that turns the scales. Just as it turns all worldly prosperity to dirt, so it turns all worldly adversities into feathers.

17. *Man*

What is man to God? What is mankind that God should be mindful of it? Vanity seems to be the lightest thing that the Holy Spirit could name, and he says over and over that "all is vanity." When the Spirit weighs man with vanity, though, he finds man lighter than vanity. The Spirit says, "Take great men and mean men all together, and they are altogether lighter than vanity." How poor and inconsiderable a rag of this world is man? If they were taken all together, all humanity would not have the power of one angel. All humanity together would not have the power of one finger of God's hand. When David said of man, "I am a worm and no man," he might have gone lower. For man is much less than a worm, since worms will eat his body in the grave and an immortal worm will gnaw upon his conscience in the torments of hell.

18. *The World a House*

Think of the entire world as a single house. Then reflect upon this house as the dwelling place of the peaceful harmony of creatures and the peace of nature. Think of this kingdom of nature as the best room in the house, whose walls are the Church and the State, royal peace and religious wisdom. Let your family be a cabinet in this room, and the boxes in this cabinet will be filled with the duties of your wife, children, and servants, the peace of virtue and active discretion and passive obedience. Your own heart is the secret box reserved for the most precious jewel in the best cabinet in the best room of the best house. In your heart you will treasure peace with nature, peace in the Church, peace in the State, peace in your house, and peace in your heart. This is a fair model and a lovely design of the heavenly Jerusalem where there is no object but peace.

19. *Wealth*

Wealth and riches are the metaphors the Holy Spirit happily uses to represent God and Heaven to us. "Despise not the riches of his goodness," says the Apostle. The Apostle also exclaims, "O the depth of his riches of his wisdom." The Apostle declares again, "the unsearchable riches of Christ" and "the riches of his glory." God's goodness toward us, God's grace on this earth, and God's glory ever after are all represented to us in metaphors of Riches. God's curses are accompanied by threats of poverty. He threatens weakness, war, captivity and poverty everywhere, but he never threatens people with wealth.

Ordinary poverty is a shrewd and slippery temptation. I call incorrigible those for whom begging in the streets has become a vocation (for parents raise their children to do it, indeed they almost take apprentices to it; some expert beggars teach others what to say, how to dress, how to lie, and how to cry). I must say of these beggars (in the fashion of our Savior's words, "It is not fitting to take the children's bread and cast it before dogs") that it is not fitting for them to devour any of those things that belong to the truly poor. There is no proportion of riches that exposes man so naturally to sin as this kind of beggary. Rich men forget or neglect the duties of their baptism, but how many of these beggars were never baptized? Rich men sleep during the sermons, but these beggars never come to church. Rich men are negligent in practice, but these beggars are ignorant of all knowledge.

It would take me a longer time than I have now to discuss whether wealth or poverty (considered in lesser proportions, ordinary riches, ordinary poverty) opens us to more or worse sins. When you consider abundant wealth and beggarly poverty, you will undoubtedly admit that the incorrigible beggar is farther from all goodness than the most corrupt rich person. Therefore, we labor earnestly in the way of some lawful calling so we may have our portion of this world by good means.

20. *Sickness*

Of all the miseries that people experience, sickness is greater than any of them. It is the immediate sword of God. Phalaris invented a bull, and others have invented torture machines such as wheels and racks. No persecutor could ever invent a sickness or a way to inflict sickness on a condemned person.

The executioner can send the condemned person to the gallows and command the hour of the condemned's death. But the executioner cannot sentence the condemned to fever or to a gout. In poverty I lack things and in banishment I lack the company of other people, but in sickness I lack my self. So, just as the greatest misery of war is when it is fought in your own country, so the greatest misery of sickness is that my own body is the subject of the afflictions. How shall I put a just value upon God's great blessings of wine, milk, and honey, when I cannot taste them, or of liberty, when gout has put my feet in chains?

21. *Joy*

Joy is the peace that comes from having done the things we ought to have done. To have something to do, to do it, to rejoice in having done it, to embrace a calling and to perform the duties of that calling, this is Christianly done, Christ did it; Godly done, God did it.

22. *Women*

Some men, out of irritability and impetuosity, have called into question the abilities and faculties of women, even wondering whether or not women have immortal souls. Perhaps these men have these doubts because St. Ambrose, in his commentaries on St. Paul's epistles, teaches that women were not created according to God's image. However, no serious author of piety who interprets the Scriptures could doubt that women were created in God's image and do indeed possess a rational and immortal soul.

The faculties and abilities of the soul appear best in matters of government and in matters of religion. We have examples of able women in both of these areas. In government matters, we have Queen Elizabeth, who any former King cannot equal. In matters of religion women have had great influence, negatively and positively. Sometimes their abundant wealth, their personal affections for some churchmen, their irregular and indiscreet zeal have made them assistants to heretics: Helena to Simon Magus, Lucilla to Donatus, another to Mahomet, others to others. But they have also been great instruments for the advance of religion, as St. Paul testifies on behalf "of the chief women, not a few" at Thessalonica.

If women have submitted themselves to as good an education as men, their should be no prejudice against them merely because of their sex. Neither their sex nor their sins should prejudice us anyone against them, for, as St. Jerome says, of all the women named in Christ's genealogy in the Gospel there is not one (except his only Blessed Virgin Mother) upon whom there does not rest some suspicion of incontinence. But of such women Christ deigned to come. He was born of woman, so that he was born of nothing but woman, not of man. Neither do we read in the Gospels of any women who assisted in Christ's persecutions or contributed to his afflictions. Even Pilate's wife dissuaded him from persecuting Christ. Woman, as well as man, was made in the image of God, in the Creation. In the Resurrection, when we will rise such as we were here, her sex will not diminish her glory.

23. *The Skin*

"Corruption in the skin," says Job. In the outward beauty of our own skins are the evidence and the records that will condemn us on the last day. We have the book of God, the Law, written in our hearts; we have the image of God imprinted in our souls; we have the character and seal of God stamped in us in our baptism. All this is bound in this parchment, in this skin of ours, and we neglect book, image, and character and seal all for the covering. If we consider the aptness of the words that "Absalom was hanged by the hair of the head," we will see that interpreters have used this verse to decry the evil of cherishing and curling hair, especially as it leads to the entangling of others. Pliny says that when thin silk clothes were first invented in Rome, it was just an occasion for women to go naked in their clothes since their skin could be seen through those thin coverings. Beloved, a good diet makes the best complexion, and a good conscience is a continual feast. A cheerful heart makes the best blood, and peace with God is true cheerfulness of heart. Your Savior neglected his skin so much that at the end of his life he had scarcely any because it had been torn by whips. Your skin will come to that absolute corruption so that one hundred years after you are buried none may say, based upon the relic of your skin, that this was a handsome person. Corruption seizes the skin and all outward beauty quickly as it does the entire body.

"If the whole body were an eye, or an ear, where were the body," says St. Paul. But when of the whole body there is neither eye nor ear nor any member left, where is the body? And what would an eye do in the grave, where it can see nothing but the repulsive? What good would a nose be in the grave, when it can smell only decay? What good would an ear be in the grave where they do not praise God? Doesn't the body, which bragged yesterday that it only could walk upright, today lie as flat upon the earth as any other creature? Painters have presented to us with some horror the skeleton, but no pencil can show us the state of the body in its decay in the grave.

24. *Satan's Small Change*

Indifferent looking, equal and easy conversation, proneness to lustful discourses, are the Devil's coins, and many of these coins make up an adultery. As light a thing as a spangle is, a spangle is silver; and leaf-gold, that is blown away, is gold; and sand that has no strength, yet coheres in a building; so approaches to sin become sin. To avoid these spots is that whiteness that God loves in the soul. But there is a redness that God loves, too, an aptness in the soul to blush when any of these spots fall upon it.

25. *Loving Christ*

Love him then; love the Lord, love Christ, love Jesus. When you look upon him as Lord and you find frowns and wrinkles on his face, you may see him as a Judge and fear him. But do not run away from him; look upon his face and let that fear bring you love. As he is Lord, you will see him in the beauty and loveliness of his creatures and in that harmony of peace between him and your soul. As he is the Lord, you will fear him, but if a person truly fears God, then that fear ends in love.

Love him as he is the Lord who wants nothing he has made to perish. Love him as he is Christ, for he has made himself human, so that humanity will not die. Love him as the Lord who can show mercy. Love him as Christ who is the way of mercy the Lord has chosen. Return again and again to that mysterious person, Christ.

I love my Savior as he is the Lord, who works for my salvation, and as Christ, who makes possible my salvation. But when I see him as Jesus accomplishing my salvation by actual death, I see those hands stretched out to the heavens and those feet wracked with pain. I hear him, from whom his nearest friends ran, pray for his enemies. I see him, forsaken by his Father, refuse to forsake his brothers. I see him who clothes his body with the flesh of his creature and his soul with Righteousness hang naked upon the Cross. I hear him who is *the Fountain of the water of life* cry out that *he thirsts*. When I contemplate my Savior in this way, I love the Lord, and there is a reverent adoration in that love. I love Christ, and there is a mysterious admiration in that love. I love Jesus, and there is a tender compassion in that love. I am content to suffer with him, and to suffer for him, rather than to see any diminishing of his glory because of my falseness.

26. *Work and the World*

Is the world a great and harmonious Organ, where all parts are played and all play a part? Must you simply sit idle and listen to it? Is everybody else made to be a Member and to do some real work to sustain this great Body, this World? Will you be the only one who is not a member of this great Body? Do you think that you were made to be a Mole in the Face for Ornament, a Man of delight in the World? Because your wit, your fashion, and some such nothing as that has made you such a delightful and acceptable companion, will you simply pass through life in jest, and be nothing? If you will not be a link in God's Chain, you will not have a part of God's providence. Since it is because of your sin that God has cursed the Earth, and that it must produce Thorns and Thistles, aren't you going to stoop down, risk pricking your hand, and weed them? Do you think you can eat bread without sweating to produce it? Do you have a prerogative above Nature's Law? Should God insert a particular clause of exemption just for your sake?

27. *God's House of Prayer*

God's House is the house of Prayer. It is his Court of Requests. There he receives petitions and acts on them. You come to God in his House as though you came to keep him company and talk with him for half an hour. Or, you come as Ambassadors, as though you have come from as great a Prince as he. You meet others and you make your bargains for your consuming greed, and then you come here to prayers and make God your Broker. You engage in robbery, extortion, bribery, and deceit, and then you come here and give to God these spoiled goods. You make God's house a den of thieves. His house is the holiest of holies, but you make it only a sanctuary. It should be a place sanctified by your devotions, and you make it only a sanctuary to protect criminals, a place that may redeem you from people's bad opinions, who are bound to think well of you because they see you here.

28. *Love*

In Divinity, Love is such an attribute that assigns to us one person of the Trinity to communicate and apply to us the two other persons. That person is the Holy Spirit. Just as there is no power but in relation to the Father, and no wisdom but in relation to the Son, there is no love but in relation to the Holy Spirit, from whom comes this purity of heart. For the love of this purity is part of this purity itself, and no person has it, except that he loves this purity. All love directed to lower things can be satisfied, but this love of purity always grows. It not only files off the rust of our hearts as it cleanses us of old habits, but it also polishes daily our hearts so that you may see your face in your heart and that the world may see your heart in your face. This purity of heart can only be preserved by this noble and incorruptible affection of Love, that values it truly and prefers it above all other things.

29. *Joy*

The person who rejoices in God has a fountain of joy. That which Christ says to the soul at the last Judgment, *Enter into your master's joy*, he says to your conscience now. The everlastingness of joy is the blessedness of the next life, and the entering into joy is the pleasure afforded the Christian life here.

30. *Prayer*

It may be mental, for we think prayers. It may be vocal, for we speak prayers. It may be actual, for we do prayers. So then to do the work of your calling sincerely is to pray. Since every righteous person is the temple of the Holy Spirit, when the person prays it is the Holy Spirit that prays. And what can be denied, when the Asker gives? He plays with us, as with children, shows us pleasant things so we might ask for them and have them. Before we call, he answers, and when we speak he hears. Doctors sometimes observe symptoms so violent that they must neglect the disease for a while and cure the symptoms. So in the sinful consumption of the soul an indisposition to prayer must first be cured. We may absolutely plead for things absolutely good, like the remission of sins, and to escape things absolutely evil, like sin. But we must ask conditionally, always deferring to the giver's will, for mean and indifferent things.

I would also rather make short prayers rather than long ones, even though God can neither be taken by surprise nor assailed. Long prayers contain more of the person, desire to be eloquent, a complacency in the work, and many distractions because of the Devil. For in long prayers, once we have pleaded for God to listen to us, we speak no more to him.

31. *Heaven*

Heaven is here, in God's Church, in his Word, in his Sacraments and in his Laws. Set your heart upon the Promise of the Gospel and you possess that treasure which is your life.

32. *True Knowledge*

Blessed are the ones whose knowledge is consummated in Jesus Christ. The University is a Paradise; Rivers of knowledge are there, and the Arts and Sciences flow from there. But the *waters of rest* that the Prophet speaks about flow out of this good Master and flow into him again. All knowledge that begins but does not end with his glory is nothing but an elaborate and exquisite ignorance.

33. *The Church is a Company*

The key of David opens and shuts; the Spirit of Comfort shines upon us and cannot be extinguished. A Church is a Company; Religion is a Religation, a binding of people together in one manner of Worship. Worship is an exterior service, and that service is to come and rejoice in God's presence.

34. *Prayer*

Prayer is our whole service to God. Earnest prayer has the nature of appeal. We press, we invoke God in Prayer. Yet God does not reject our prayers just because of that. God tolerates our entreaty and puts up with our impudence. We threaten God in prayer, as Gregory of Nazianus tells us. His sister, he says, would threaten God in the fury of her prayer. She would threaten God, and tell him that she would never leave his altar until he had granted her petitions. And God tolerates this impudence and even more. Prayer has the nature of violence. In the public prayers of the Congregation, we assail God, said Tertullian, and we take God prisoner and bring him to our conditions. God is glad to be straightened by us in

that siege. The Prophet executes what the Apostle later rec-
ommends, *Pray incessantly.* Even in his singing he prays. As St.
Basil says, "A Good man's dreams are Prayers." He prays in
his sleep, and thus David's songs are Prayers.

35. *Unconscious Prayer*

The soul accustomed to directing herself to God on every
occasion, like a flower at the sunrise, spreads and dilates
toward him in thankfulness for every small blessing he sheds
on her. This soul, like a flower at sunset, gathers into herself
as though she had received a blow when she hears her Savior
maligned by blasphemy. This soul, whatever chord is struck in
her, is always tuned toward God, and this soul prays some-
times when she does not realize she prays.

36. *God's Image*

Our Savior Christ, whose every drop of blood was of infi-
nite value (for one of our souls is worth more than the entire
world, and one drop of his blood, if it had been applied to
them, would have been sufficient for all the souls of 1,000
worlds) was sold scornfully and basely at a low price. We sell
our selves, and him too, and we crucify him again every day,
for nothing. When our sin is the very crucifying of sin that
should save us, who will save us? Earthly princes have been
so jealous of their honor that they have made it treasonous to
carry their pictures irreverently into any places not worthy of
their honor. Whenever we commit any sin, whether purposeful
or not, the image of God, which is engraved and imprinted in
us, is mingled with that sin. We draw the image of God into
all our intemperance; we carry his image into all the foul
places we haunt on the earth. We even carry his image down
with us to eternal condemnation, for, as Saint Bernard says,
*The image of God burns us in hell, but can never be burned out of
us.* As long as the understanding soul remains, the image of

God remains in it. We have used the image of God as witches are said to use the images of men; by melting the image, they destroy the person. By defacing God's image in ourselves by sin, we bring it to the painful and shameful death of the Cross.

37. *The Soul of Law*

Determining how far human law binds the conscience and how far it lays such an obligation upon us that if we violate it we incur a penalty but also sin toward God, has been a perplexing question in all times and places. However diverse opinion is, though, all interpreters agree that no law can be merely a human law; it also has in it a divine part. There is in every human law part of the law of God, which is obedience to the superior. It might be good to argue that man cannot bind the conscience because he can neither judge the conscience nor absolve the conscience. But in the laws made by the power ordained in God, man does not bind the conscience, for only God can do so. Then you must be the subject, not because of wrath but because of conscience. Though the matter and subject of the law, that which the law commands or prohibits, may be an indifferent action, in all these God has his part. There is a certain divine soul and spark of God's power that goes through all laws and animates them.

38. *Sin's Body*

There is in us a heart of sin that must be cast up. While the heart is under the habits of sin, we are not only sinful, but we are all sin, just as it is truly said that land flooded with sea is all sea. When sin is in our heart, it will quickly come to be that entire body of death, as Saint Paul says, *Who shall deliver me from the Body of this Death?* When it is a heart, it will get a brain that will delight in sin. A brain will send forth sinews and ligaments to tie sins together and marrow to give nourishment even to those bones that give strength to sin. It will do all those services for sin that it does for the natural body. If sin gets to be a heart, it will get a liver to carry blood and life through all the body of our sinful actions, for that's the liver's office. While we argue whether the seat of the soul is in the heart, brain or liver, this tyrant sin will dominate all and become all. We will find nothing in us without sin, nothing in us but sin, if our heart is inhabited and possessed by it.

39. *Small Sins*

Whoever possesses purity of heart and wishes to preserve it will sweep down every cobweb that hangs about it. Indecent and obscene language, pleasurable conversation, and all such little entanglements, which he thinks are too weak to hold him, indeed foul his soul. Whoever is subject to these smaller sins should remember that just as a spider always builds where it knows there are the most flies, so the Devil has cast these light cobwebs into your heart because he knows the heart is made of vanities. He who gathers into his treasure whatever you waste out of your treasure, he will produce against you as many lascivious glances as will make up an adultery, as many covetous wishes as make up a robbery, and as many angry words as will make up a murder. You will have dropped away your soul, with as much irrecoverableness as if you had poured it out all at once. Your merry sins will grow to be crying sins, even in God's ears. Although you drown your soul here, drop after drop, it will not burn spark after spark, but have all the fire, and all at once, and all eternally, in one entire and intense torment.

40. *Salvation Sure*

What soul among us doubts that when God has such an abundant and infinite treasure in the passion of Jesus Christ, sufficient to save millions, that many millions in this world are excluded from his interest? Who doubts that God has a kingdom so large that it has no limits, but he has banished from his kingdom many natural subjects, even those legions of angels that were created in it and fallen from it? What soul among us doubts that he who has so much and loves so much will not deny her a portion in the blood of Christ or a room in the kingdom of heaven?

He sought you among the infinite numbers of false and fashionable Christians, so he might separate you from the hypocrites to serve him earnestly in holiness and righteousness. He sought you among the herd of the Gentiles, who had no Church, to bring you into his gates and pastures, his visible Church, and to feed you with his word and his sacraments. He sought you in the catalogue of all his creatures, where he might have left you a stone, or a plant, or an animal. He then gave you an immortal soul, capable of all his future blessings. He sought you when you were nowhere and nothing, and he brought you from being nothing to being a creature. How early did he seek you? He sought you in Adam's confused loins, and out of that leavened and sour loaf in which we were all kneaded up, out of that mass of damnation, that condemned lump of dough, he sought out that grain that you should be. Millions and millions of generations before this he sought you in his own eternal decree. In that first scripture of his, which is as old as he, in that book of life he wrote your name in the blood of that Lamb which was sacrificed for you, not only from the beginning of this world but from the writing of that eternal decree of salvation. So, very early he sought you in the Church among hypocrites, outside the Church among the heathens, in his creatures among creatures of an ignoble nature, and in the first emptiness, when you were nothing, he sought you in Adam and in the book of life. When do you think the time is right to seek him?

41. *Sects*

Sects are not bodies, but they are rotten boughs, diseased limbs blown off by their own turbulent spirit, fallen off by the weight of their own pride, or sawed off by the censures and excommunications of the Church. Sects are no bodies, for there is nothing in common among them, nothing that goes through them all. All is singular; all is my spirit and your spirit, my opinion and your opinion, and my God and your God. The entire Church is not acquainted with such worship.

It is true that every person must appropriate God so narrowly as to find him to be his own God. He must make his own all the promises of the prophets, all the performances of the Gospel, all that Jesus Christ said and did and suffered. Yet God is my God just as he is our God, just as I am part of that Church, with which he has promised to be until the end of the world, and as I am an obedient son of that mother, who is the spouse of Jesus Christ.

CHAPTER III
Prayers

I.   O eternal and most gracious God, as we consider you in your-
self, you are a circle, first and last, and altogether. As we con-
sider your workings upon us, you are a direct line and lead us
from our beginning, through all our ways, to our end. Enable
me by your grace to look forward to my end and to look back-
ward to reflect upon the mercies you have given me from the
beginning. So, from my practice of reflecting on your mercy
in my beginning in this world, when you planted me in the
Christian church, and your mercy in the beginning in the
other world, when you write my name in the book of life, I
may come to a holy consideration of all my actions here. In all
the beginnings of spiritual sickness of sin, may I hear that
voice, "O man of God, there is death in the pot," and so avoid
that to which I was hungrily flying. "A faithful ambassador is
health," says the wise Solomon. Received in the beginning of
a sickness, of a sin, your voice is true health. If I can see that
light and hear that voice, "Then my light shall break forth as
the morning, and my health shall spring forth speedily."
Deliver me, therefore, O my God, from these vain imagina-
tions. Assure me that you will speak to me at the beginning
of every spiritual sickness and sin. If I recognize your voice
and fly to you, you will keep me from falling, or raise me up
again when I have fallen because of my natural weakness. Do
this, O Lord, for the sake of the One who knows our weak-
nesses, for he had them, and knows the weight of our sins, for
he paid a dear price for them, your Son, our Savior, Christ
Jesus. Amen.

II. O Most Gracious God, who pursue and perfect your own pur-
poses, you remind me, by the beginnings of my illness, that I
must die. You inform me as the sickness progresses that I may
die today. You have not only walked with me from the first,
but you have called me up to you by casting me down into
sickness. You have clothed me with yourself by stripping me
of my self. By dulling my bodily senses to the eases of this
world, you have sharpened my spiritual senses so I can grasp
you. Quicken the pace of the steps you take, my God, to dis-
solve this body of mine and multiply those degrees in the exal-
tation of my soul toward you. My taste is not gone away, but
gone to sit at David's table, "to taste and see that the Lord is
good." My stomach is not gone, but it is gone so far upwards
toward the "supper of the Lamb" with your saints in heaven
and to the communion of your saints here on earth. My knees
are weak so that I should easily fall to them and concentrate
on my devotions to you. "A sound heart is the life of the
flesh," and a heart that you visit and direct to you is a sound
heart. "There is no rest in my bones, because of my sin."
Transfer my sins, with which you are so displeased, to Christ
Jesus, with whom you are well pleased, and there will be a rest
in my bones. My God, appear to me in the midst of these
brambles and sharp thorns of my sickness so I may see you
and know you are my God. Do this, O Lord, for the sake of
the One who was no less the King of heaven because he was
crowned with thorns in this world.

III. Most mighty and most merciful God, though you have taken
me off my feet, you have not removed me from my founda-
tion, which is you. Although you have dislodged me from that
standing form in which I could see your throne, the heavens,
you have not taken from me the light by which I can lie and
see myself. Even though you have weakened my bodily knees
so they cannot bow to you, you have left me the knees of my

heart, which are bowed to you forever. Just as you have made this bed your altar, make me your sacrifice. Just as you have made your Son, Jesus Christ, the priest, so make me his deacon, to minister to him in a cheerful surrender of body and soul. I come unto you, my God, so I can come to you by embracing your coming to me. I come to you, thinking confidently of David's promise, "that you will sustain me in my sickness." So, whichever way I turn I feel your hand upon my body, and your hand disciplines and rewards me at the same time. Just as you have made the feathers of this bed the thorns of my sickness, O Lord, now turn these thorns into feathers again, like the feathers of your dove, and make them instruments of true comfort. Do not take advantage of my illness, God, to terrify my soul by saying, "Now I have met you where you have so often departed from my ways." But, having burnt up this bed of idleness with burning fevers and washed it in these drenching sweats, make my bed again, O Lord, and enable me "to commune with my own heart upon my bed, and be still." Enable me to provide a bed for all my former sins while I lie on this bed, and a grave for my sins before I come to my grave. When I have laid my sins in the Son's wounds, enable me to rest in the assurance that my conscience is discharged from further anxiety and my soul from further danger. Do this, O Lord, for the sake of your Son, our Savior, Jesus Christ, who did and suffered so much that in your justice and mercy you might do for me.

IV. O mightiest and most merciful God, you are so much the God of health and strength that without you all health is nothing but the fuel of sin. Look at me, for I am afflicted by the ardor of two diseases, and I need two doctors, the bodily and the spiritual physician. I bless and glorify your name because you have given help to humans by the ministry of humans. Even in heaven itself, you have planted a tree that is "a tree of life, but the leaves are for the healing of the nations." Life itself is with you there, for you are life itself. All kinds of health descend from there. "You would have healed Babylon, but she is not healed." Remove from me, Lord, her perverseness and her willfulness; hear your Spirit say to my soul: "Heal me, O Lord, for I want to be healed." Keep me away, Lord, from those who falsely profess the art of healing the soul or body by means not implanted by you in the church, for the soul, and in nature, for the body. Spiritual health cannot be gotten by superstition, nor bodily health by witchcraft. Lord, you and only you are the Lord of both. You in yourself are Lord of both, and, in your Son, you are the physician, the applier of bodily and spiritual health. How much more will I now be healed when that which Christ has already suffered is applied effectually to me? Is there any vein so empty that his blood cannot fill it? When the inhabitants of the earth pray that you heal the earth, you promise to heal it. You promise to heal their waters, but "You will not heal their miry places." Thus, my return to sin and my ability to perform all sins over again you will not pardon. "Your Son went about healing all manner of sickness." "Virtue went out of him, and he healed all," all the multitude, and he left no trace of the disease. Will this universal physician pass by this hospital and not visit me and not heal me completely? If I must die this day that days shall be no more, give to me my spiritual health through the work of your church. Allow your teachings to flourish through those who treat my bodily sickness so that they may glorify you and edify those who observe the issues given by your servants.

V. O eternal and most gracious God, you called down fire from heaven upon the sinful cities only once; you opened the earth to swallow the murmurers only once; you threw down the tower of Siloam on sinners only once. But repeat your works of mercy often, and work by your own patterns, just as you brought man into this world. So, whether it is your will to let me live or to dismiss me by death, please give me the help I need for both conditions, either for my weak stay here or for my final migration away from here. Glorify yourself, if you may receive glory in this way, by preserving this body from infections that would keep visitors away or endanger them. Preserve this soul from all questions that might shake the assurance that I and others have had that you would love me to my death and even at my death. Do not open the doors of my heart, my ears, my house to any that would enter to undermine my faith in you. Be my salvation and plead my salvation; work it and declare it, and let the church be assured that you were my God and I was your servant, even until death. I wrap all these requests in two petitions—"Thy kingdom come, thy will be done." Amen.

VI. O most mighty and merciful God, the God of all true sorrow and true joy, of all fear and all hope, as you have given me a repentance, so give me a fear of which I am not afraid. Give me tender and supple affections so that I rejoice with those who rejoice, mourn with those who mourn, and fear with those who fear. Since fear accompanies me in this sickness, help me not to lose the fitting sense of fear that helps me prepare for the worst that may be feared, my death. Many of the blessed martyrs have passed out of this life without showing any fear, but your most blessed Son did not do so. Your martyrs were but men, so it pleased you to fill them with your Spirit and power. Your Son declared himself to be God, but he also declared himself to be human and to take on human weakness. Let me not be afraid of these fears, God, but let me feel them as Christ did so I may submit all, as he did, to your will. When you have thawed my former coldness and lack of devotion with these fevers, and when you have quenched my former heats with these fevers and sweats and made right my former negligences with these fears, you may be pleased, God, to think I am fit for you. Whether you dispose of this body, this garment, by asking me to wear it further in this world or by laying it in the common wardrobe, the grave, glorify yourself with the glory that your Son, our Savior, Jesus Christ, has purchased for the ones who partake of Christ's resurrection. Amen.

VII. O eternal and most gracious God, you provided manna in the wilderness so that to every person the manna tasted like that which he or she liked best. I humbly ask you to conform my taste to yours so that your admonishments, part of my daily bread, taste as you would have them taste. Your admonishments taste of humiliation, but they taste of consolation, too. They taste of danger, but also of assurance. You have imprinted in our bodies two qualities, so that as fire dries, it also heats, and as water moistens, it also cools. Your admonishments, Lord, are elements of our rebirth, by which our souls become yours; imprint your two qualities so they may chasten us into the path toward you. You have let me see in just a few hours how you can place me beyond man's help; let me by that same light see that no feverish sickness, no temptation of Satan, no guiltiness of sin, no prison of death, neither this sick bed, nor the grave can remove me from the determined and good purpose that you have secured for me. Do not let me think that your admonishments are casual or without meaning. When I have understood this sickness as an admonishment, I also understand it as your mercy. Whether your original intention in this sickness was admonishment or mercy, I cannot determine, although death determines for me. For as it must appear as an admonishment, I can have no greater argument for your mercy than to die in you and by that death to be united to him who died for me.

VIII.   O eternal and most gracious God, you have reserved your treasure of perfect joy and perfect glory to distribute yourself. By seeing you as you are in yourself and knowing you as we know ourselves, we will possess in an instant and forever all that can in any way promote our happiness. In this world, give us such a pledge of that full payment that by the value of the pledge we may have some estimate of the treasure. As we see you here in a mirror, so we receive from you in this world by reflection and by instruments. Even casual things come from you. What we call fortune here has another name above. Nature reaches out her hand and gives us corn, wine, oil, and milk. You fill her hand before and you open her hand so she may rain down her showers upon us. Industry reaches out her hand and gives us fruits of our labors for ourselves and our children. Your hand guides that hand when it plants and when it waters, and the growth is from you. Friends reach out their hands and prefer us, but your hand supports the hands that support us. I have received blessings from all these instruments, O God. But I bless your name most for the greatest blessing, that by your powerful hand set over us I have had my portion in the hearing and the preaching of the Gospel. I humbly ask that you will continue your known goodness to the entire world by the same recognized nature and industry. So continue the same blessings upon this state and this church by the same hand. When your Son comes in the clouds, may the Son find me, or my son, or my son's sons ready to give an account for their faithful stewardship and dispensation of your talents you so abundantly committed to them. Be to this preacher, O God, in all the fevers of his body, in all the anxieties of spirit, in all holy sadnesses of soul, a physician, the greatest in heaven, as Christ has been my physician on this earth.

IX. O eternal and most gracious God, your eyes are so pure you can-
not look upon sin. We are of such impure constitutions that we
can present no object other than sin to you. We justly fear,
then, that you would turn your eyes away from us forever. We
cannot endure afflictions ourselves, but through you we can.
Though you cannot endure sin in us, your Son can, and he
has taken upon himself and presented to you all our sins that
might displease you. The eye of a serpent kills as soon as it
sees. No eye in nature nourishes us by looking at us. But your
eye, O Lord, does nourish us. Look upon me, O Lord, in my
distress, and your look will recall me from the borders of this
bodily death. Look upon me, and that will raise me again
from that spiritual death in which my parents buried me
when they conceived me in sin. I have entered the jaws of hell
by heaping numerous actual sins upon the foundation of
original sin. Take me again into your counsel, blessed and
glorious Trinity. The Father knows I have defaced his image
received in creation, and the Son knows I have neglected my
interest in redemption. Blessed Spirit, testify to them that at
this moment I accept Your blessed inspirations which I have
so often rebelliously rejected. Be my witness that this sad
soul weeps blood out of more pores than it sweats tears.
Take me into your counsel, then, O blessed and glorious
Trinity, and prescribe medicine for me. If it is a long and
painful holding of this soul in sickness, it is nonetheless
medicine if I may discern your hand in it. If it is to be a
speedy departing of this soul, it is medicine if I may discern
your hand will receive it.

X. O eternal and most gracious God, you know all my sins when
I confess them to you. How can I tell you, then, those sins
that I don't know about? If I accuse myself of original sin, will
you ask me if I know what original sin is? I do not know
enough of it to satisfy others, but I know enough to condemn

myself, and to ask your guidance. If I confess to you the sins of my youth, will you ask me if I know what those sins were? I do not know them so well as to name them all (for I did them faster than I can speak them now, when every thing I did promoted some sin), but I know them so well as to know that nothing but your mercy is as infinite as my sin. If the naming of sins of thought, word, and deed, of sins of omission and of action, of sins against you, my neighbor, and myself, of sins unrepented and relapsed into after repentance, of sins of ignorance and sins against the testimony of my conscience, of sins against your commandments, sins against your Son's Prayer, sins against our own creed, of sins against laws of that church and sins against the laws of the state in which you have given me my place do not name all my sins, I know what will. O Lord, pardon me for all those sins which your Son, Jesus Christ, suffered for. He suffered for all the sins of the world, and there is no sin among all those that would not be my sin. Since sin retains so much of its author that it is a serpent, insinuating itself into my soul, let your bold serpent (the contemplation of your Son crucified for me) be forever present to me, for my recovery against the sting of the first serpent. So I may have a serpent against a serpent, the wisdom of the serpent against the malice of the serpent as well as humility and peace and reconciliation to you, by the laws of your church. Amen.

XI. O eternal and most gracious God, in your upper house, your heavens, you are equally in every mansion, even though there are many mansions. But here in your lower house, you are in some rooms and not in others. You are more in your church than in my chamber, and more in your sacraments than in my prayers. So even though you are always present and always working in every room of this your house, my body, I humbly ask you to occupy my heart more than any other room.

Traitors and disloyal people will come into the house of your anointed; hypocrites and idolators will come into your house, the church; temptations and infections will come into some rooms of this your house, my body. But let my heart be your chamber, O God, and do not let them enter there. Job made a covenant with his eyes, but your dwelling in his heart enabled him to keep that covenant. Your Son himself had a sadness in his soul about his death, and he regretted its approach. But he possessed his medicine, too: *Yet not my will, but yours be done.* Just as you have not delivered us, your adopted children, from these infectious temptations, you have not delivered us over to them nor withheld your medicine from us. I was baptized in your medicinal water against original sin, and I have drunk of your medicinal blood, for my recovery from actual and habitual sin. O Lord, you who have imprinted all medicinal virtues that are in all creatures are able to make this present sickness, everlasting health, this weakness, everlasting health, and this faintness of heart, a powerful balm. When your blessed Son cried out to you, *My God, my God, why have you forsaken me?* you reached out your hand to him, not to deliver his sad soul but to receive his holy soul. I see your hand on me now, O Lord, and I do not ask what it intends. Infirmity of nature and curiosity of mind are temptations, but a silent and absolute obedience to your will, even before I know your will, is my medicine. When you have catechized me with affliction here, I will be able to take a greater degree and serve you in a higher place, in your kingdom of joy and glory. Amen.

XII. O eternal and most gracious God, you have permitted us to destroy ourselves, but you have not given us the power to repair ourselves. You have given us a means of repair that we may easily understand. I humbly ask you that you will allow to flourish this means of bodily assistance in your ordinary

creature and allow to flourish your means of spiritual assis-
tance in your holy laws. As you have carried the dove through
nature, making it medicinally helpful to our bodily health,
through the law, making it a sacrifice for sin there, through
the gospel, making it, and your spirit in it, a witness to your
Son's baptism, so carry it home to my soul and imprint there
the simplicity, mildness, and harmlessness you have imprinted
by nature in this creature. Since all disobedience to you is sub-
dued beneath my feet, I may, in the power and triumph of the
Son, tread victoriously on my grave. In the words of your
prophet, O Lord, the dove is called the *dove of the valleys*, but
You promise that the *dove of the valleys shall be upon the moun-
tain*. As you have laid me low in this valley of sickness, so, in
your good time carry me up to these mountains which even
in this valley I can see. Carry me up to that mountain where
You dwell, where no one can ascend *but he that has clean
hands*, which none can have but by that one way of cleansing
them, in the blood of your Son, Jesus Christ. Amen.

XIII. O eternal and most gracious God, you give all for nothing.
Accept my humble thanks, both for your mercy and for this
particular mercy, that in your judgments I can discern your
mercy and find comfort in Your admonishments. I know, O
Lord, the discomfort that accompanies the phrase that the
house is visited and your marks are upon the patient. But
what a wretched hermitage that is that is not visited by you,
and what an orphan is that person who does not bear your
marks. These fevers, O Lord, that you have brought upon my
body are but your chafing of the wax that you might seal me
to you. These spots are simply the letters in which you have
written your own name and revealed yourself to me. Be ever
present to me, O my God, and this chamber and yours will be
all one room. The closing of the bodily eyes here and the
opening of my soul's eyes there will be all one act.

XIV. O eternal and most gracious God, even though you created darkness before light in Creation, you so multiplied that light that it illuminated the day and the night. Though you have permitted some clouds of sadness to darken my soul, I humbly bless and glorify your holy name, for you have permitted me the light of the Spirit, against which the prince of darkness cannot prevail nor hinder the illumination of our darkest nights or saddest thoughts. Even the visitation of your most blessed Spirit upon the blessed Virgin is called an overshadowing. There was the presence of the Holy Spirit, the fountain of all light, and yet an overshadowing. Unless there were some light, there could be no shadow. Let your merciful providence govern all this sickness so I never fall into utter darkness or ignorance of you. Let those shadows that do fall upon me be overcome by the power of your irresistible light, the God of consolation. If I should fall into darkness, let the Spirit do his work upon those shadows and disperse them. Situate me in such a bright day here that the words of your Son, spoken to his apostles, may reflect upon me: *Behold, I am with you always, even to the end of the world.*

XV. O Eternal God, you granted your servant Abraham one prayer as an encouragement to offer another prayer. I implore you, then, since I have meditated upon you and spoken of you for such a long time, to let me speak to you. Since you have enlightened me to contemplate your greatness, O God, now descend to look at my infirmities and the Egypt in which I live. Expedite my Exodus and deliverance, for I desire to be dissolved and to be with you. O Lord, I most humbly acknowledge and confess your infinite Mercy. When you had called a famine of your word upon almost the entire world, you brought me into this Egypt, where you had appointed your servants to harvest your blessings and to feed your flock. Here also, O God, you have multiplied your children in me, because you have taught me to cherish reverent devotions to you and to enact pious affections toward you. Even so, my own corruption continues to smother and strangle those affections. You have placed me along my path toward your land of promise, your heavenly Canaan, by removing me from the Egypt of populous places. You have placed me in a more solitary and deserted place where I may more safely feed upon your Manna, which is your body in your sacrament. You have also given me the true angel's food, contemplation of you. O Lord, I most humbly acknowledge and confess that I feel the strong effects of your Power. But since they are so ordinary and so frequent they cannot be called Miracles. For every hour you remedy my lameness; every hour you restore my sight; every hour you not only deliver me from Egypt but also raise me from the death of sin. My sin, O God, has not only caused your descent and passion here, but by my sin I also become that hell into which you descended after your Passion. Every hour you in your Spirit descend into my heart to overthrow legions of spirits of Disobedience, Unbelief, and Complaining. O Lord, I most humbly acknowledge and confess that because of your Mercy I have a sense of your Justice. For those afflictions you choose to inflict upon me awaken me to just how terrible your severe justice is. But the rest and security you give me often frightens me and makes me realize that you may reserve and spare me for a greater measure of punishment. O Lord, I most humbly acknowledge and confess that I have understood sin by understanding your laws and judgments. But I have gone against your known and revealed will. You have set up many candlesticks and lit many lamps in me, but I have either blown them out or carried them to guide me in forbidden ways. You have given me a desire for knowledge, some of the means to obtain it, and some possession of it. I have armed myself with your weapons against you. Yet, O God, for your own sake have mercy on me. Do not let sin and me be able to exceed you, or defraud you, or frustrate your purposes. But let me, in spite of myself, be of so much use to your glory that because of your mercy to my sin other sinners may see just how much sin you will pardon. Show to us as much of your Judgments as will teach us and not condemn us. Hear us, O God, because of this contrition you have placed in us and by which your Son assured us of access.

XVI. O Eternal God, you are not only first and last, but you are the one in whom first and last are all one. You are not only all Mercy and all Justice, but you are the one in whom Mercy and Justice are all one. In the height of your Justice you would not spare your own and most innocent Son. In the depth of your mercy you would not have even the most wretched person meet with destruction. Behold us, O God, gathered here today in fear of you, according to your laws and confident in your promise that when two or three are gathered in your name you will be in their midst and grant them their petitions. We confess, O God, that we are not even worthy to confess, much less to be heard, least of all to be pardoned of our many sins against you. We have betrayed your Temples to profanity, our bodies to sensuality, your fortresses to your enemy, our souls to Satan. We have armed him to fight against you with your own ammunition, for we have surrendered our eyes, ears, and all our senses to his tyranny. Vanities and disguises have covered us and thus we are naked. Licentiousness has inflamed us and thus we are frozen. Voluptuousness has fed us and thus we are starved. Men's fancies and traditions have taught us, and thus we are ignorant. Only you, O God, who are true and perfect harmony, can mend our fevers and our anger. Do this, O most merciful Father, for the sake of your most innocent Son. Since he has spread his arms upon the cross to receive the entire world, O Lord, do not shut any of us out from the benefit of his merits. With as many of us who

begin their conversion and newness of life this moment, O
God, begin your account with them and put all past sins out
of memory. Accept our humble thanks for all your mercies and
continue to increase them.

XVII. O most glorious and gracious God, into whose presence
our own consciences make us afraid to come, and from whose
presence we cannot hide our selves, hide us in the wounds of
your Son, our Savior, Jesus Christ. Though our sins be as red
as scarlet, give them another redness which may be acceptable
in your sight. We renounce, O Lord, all our confidence in this
world. For this world and its lusts pass away. We renounce all
our confidence in our own merits. We renounce all confi-
dence in our confessions, for our sins are above number. We
renounce all confidence in our repentances, for we have found
that we never perfect our promises to you but relapse again
and again into those sins of which we have again and again
repented. We have no confidence in this world, but in him
who has taken possession of the next world for us by sitting
at your right hand. We have no confidence in our merits, but
in him whose merits you have been pleased to accept for us
and to apply to us. We have no confidence in our own con-
fessions and repentance but in that blessed Spirit who is the
Author of them and loves to build upon their foundations.
Accept them then, O Lord, for the sake of those to whom they
belong. Accept our poor endeavors for your glorious Son's
sake, who gives them root. Accept our poor beginnings of
sanctification, for your blessed Spirit's sake, who gives them
their growth. Accept our humble prayers for your Son's sake,
in whom only are our prayers acceptable to you, and for your
Spirit's sake which is now in us and which must be in us
whenever we pray acceptably to you.

XVIII. O Eternal and most merciful God, we know and acknowledge that we have multiplied contemptuous sins against you. We know, too, that it was even more sinful to doubt of your mercy for them. Have mercy on us. Be merciful to us in the merits and mediation of your Son, our Savior, Jesus Christ. Do not allow, O Lord, so great a waste as the emission of his blood without any return to you. Do not allow the expense of so rich a treasure as the spending of his life without any purchase to you. Just as you emptied his glory here on earth, glorify us in the kingdom of heaven with that glory that his humiliation purchased for us. As you emptied your Kingdom by banishing those Angels whose pride threw them into everlasting ruin, repair that Kingdom by assuming us into their places. To that purpose, O Lord, make us capable of that succession to your angels. Begin in us here in this life an angelic purity, an angelic chastity, an angelic integrity to your service, an angelic acknowledgment that we always stand in your presence and we should direct all our actions to your glory. Do not reprimand us in anger, O Lord, that we have not done so until now. Enable us to begin that great work. Imprint in us an assurance that you receive us now graciously, as reconciled, though enemies; fatherly, as children, though prodigals; and powerfully, as the God of our salvation, although our own consciences testify against us. Continue to increase your blessing upon the entire Church.

XIX. O eternal and most gracious God, you have consecrated our living bodies to your own Spirit and made us temples of the Holy Spirit. You alone require respect be given to these temples, even when the priest is gone out of them, and to these bodies even when the soul is departed from them. I bless and glorify your name, for as you take care of every hair on our head in life, you also take care of every grain of ashes after our death. Neither do you do only good to us all in life and death, but you would also have us do good to one another, as in a holy life. In this contemplation I make account that I hear this dead brother of ours, who is now carried out to his burial, now speak to me in the voice of these bells. In him, O God, you have carried out Dives' request to Abraham: You have sent one from the dead to speak to me. He speaks to me aloud from the steeple; he whispers to me at these curtains; he speaks your words: *Blessed are the dead which die in the Lord from this day forward.* Let this prayer, therefore, my God, be as my last gasp, my expiring, my dying in you. If this is the hour of my transmigration, may I die the death of a sinner, drowned in my sins in the blood of your Son. If I live longer, may I yet die the death of the righteous, the resurrection to a new life. "You kill and you give life": However it comes, it comes from you; however it comes, let me come to you.

XX. O eternal and most gracious God, you have joined man and woman together, made them one flesh, and you would also have them become one soul so that they might maintain a sympathy in their affections and conform to one another in the accidents of this world, good or bad. Thus having married this soul and this body in me, I humbly ask you that my soul may look and make use of your merciful proceedings toward my bodily restitution and go the same way to a spiritual restitution. I am come, by your goodness, to wash away the sinful humors that have endangered my body. I have, O Lord, a river in my body, but a sea in my soul, a sea swollen into a deluge. You have raised up certain hills in me before on which I might have stood safe from the inundations of sin. Even our natural faculties are a hill and might preserve us from some sin. Education, study, observation, and example are also hills that might preserve us some. Your church, your word, your sacraments, and your laws are hills above these other hills. Your spirit of remorse, compunction, and repentance for former sin are hills as well, and to the top of these hills you have brought me. But this deluge, this inundation, has reached above all my hills and I have sinned and sinned and multiplied sin to sin. After all your assistance against sin, where is there water enough to wash away this deluge? There is a red sea, greater than this ocean, and there is a little spring, through which this ocean may pour itself into that red sea. Let your spirit of true contrition and sorrow pass all my sins through these eyes into the wounds of your Son, and I will be clean, and my soul will be so much better purged than my body, as it is ordained for a better and a longer life.

XXI. O eternal and most gracious God, you have conveyed to us the infinite merits of your Son in the water of baptism and in the bread and wine of your other sacrament. Receive the sacrifice of my humble thanks that you have not only given me the ability to rise out of this bed of weariness and discomfort, but you have also made this bodily rising, by your grace, a promise of a second resurrection from sin, and of a third, to everlasting glory. Your Son himself, always infinite in himself, was yet pleased to grow in the Virgin's womb and to grow in stature in the sight of men. Your good purposes upon me, I know, are determined by your holy will upon me. Reveal your purposes to me in your seasons and in such measure and degree that I may not only have the comfort of knowing you to be infinitely good, but also have the comfort of finding you better and better to me every day. Give me yourself in the knowledge that whatever grace you give me today, that I should die tomorrow if I did not have tomorrow's grace as well. Thus, I beg of you my daily bread. You gave me the bread of sorrow for many days, the bread of hope for some days, and the bread of possessing in this day, in rising by that strength that you, the God of all strength, have infused in me. Lord, continue to give me the bread of life: the spiritual bread of life, in a faithful assurance in you; the sacramental bread of life, in a worthy receiving of you; the more real bread of life in an everlasting union to you. I know, Lord, that when you created angels, and they saw you produce fowl and fish, and beasts and worms, did they not ask you, "Shall we have no better creatures than these, no better companions than these?" You then had man, not much inferior to their nature, delivered over to them. No more do I, O God, now that I am able, by your mercy, to rise, question you to confirm my health. Nor do I now presume upon my spiritual strength, for by your mercy I see what your reproofs have wrought physically in me. I acknowledge that my bodily strength is subject to every puff of wind, and my spiritual strength is subject to every puff of vanity. Keep me still, therefore, O my gracious God, in such a proportion of both strengths that I may still have something to ask you for, which I have received, and still something to pray for and ask from your hand.

CHAPTER IV

Death's Duel

     Our God is a God of salvation, and to God, the Lord, belongs escape from death (Psalm 68:20).

Buildings stand because of the foundations that sustain and support them, and because of the buttresses that contain and embrace them. The foundations keep them from sinking, and the buttresses keep them from shifting. The body of our building is in the former part of this verse: *He that is our God is the God of salvation.* He is the God that gives us temporal and spiritual salvation, too. But the foundations and buttresses of this building are the latter part of the verse, and I the three diverse interpretations of the words: *To God, the Lord, belongs escape from death.* For, first, the foundation of this building (that our God is the God of all salvation) is laid in this: that to this *God the Lord belongs escape from death.* It is in his power to deliver us, even when we are brought to the jaws and teeth of death, and to the lips of that whirlpool, the grave. So, in this interpretation, this escape from death is a deliverance from death, and this is the most obvious and ordinary interpretation of these words. Second, the buttresses that keep this building from shifting, that he that is our God is the God of all salvation, must be understood. Here, *to God, the Lord, belongs escape from death,* can be interpreted regarding the disposition and manner of our death. What kind of escape and migration out of this world will we have? Will it be expected or sudden, violent or natural, in good health or in terrible sickness? There is no judgment we can make on the manner of death, for however we die, *precious in his sight is the death of his saints* and with him are the manners of death; the ways of departing are in his hands. So in this sense of the words the escape from death is a deliverance in death. God will not deliver us from dying, but he will care for us in the hour of death, whatever the manner of death might be. Finally, this God, being God and also having come into this world in our flesh, could have no other means to save us, no other means of escape from this world to return to his former glory, but by death. In this sense, this escape from death is a deliverance by death, by the death of this God, our Lord Jesus Christ. In these three lines, then, we will look upon these words: First, as the God of power, the almighty Father rescues his servants from the jaws of death; second, as the God of mercy, the glorious Son rescued us by taking upon himself the escape from death; finally, as the God of comfort, the Holy Spirit rescues us from all discomfort so whatever manner of death is ordained for us our escape from death will be an entrance into everlasting life. These three considerations—our deliverance from death, in death, and by death—will abundantly do the offices of this building, that God is the God of all salvation, for to this *God, the Lord, belongs escape from death.*

First, then, we consider this escape from death to be a deliverance from death. Therefore, in all our deaths and deadly calamities of this life, we may justly hope of a good deliverance from God. All our transitions in this life are just so many passages from death to death. Our very birth into this life is an escape from death, for in our mother's womb we are dead inasmuch as we do not know we are living. Neither is there any grave that is so pure and putrid a prison as the womb would be if we stayed in it beyond our time or died there before our time. In the womb the dead child kills the mother that conceived it and is a murderer even after it is dead. And if we are not dead in the womb, killing her that first gave us life, we are dead as David's idols are dead. In the womb we have *eyes and cannot see, ears and cannot hear.* There in the womb we are fitted for works of darkness, all the while deprived of light. There in the womb we are taught cruelty, by being fed with blood, and may be damned, though we may never be born. Of our making in the womb, David says, *I am fearfully and wonderfully made,* and *Such knowledge is too excellent for me,* for even that *is the Lord's doing, and it is wonderful in our eyes.* Job says, *Your hands have made and fashioned me round about and you have taken pains about me, yet you destroy me.* Though I am the greatest masterpiece of the great master, if you leave me where you made me and do no more for me, destruction will follow. The womb, which should be the house of life, becomes death itself if God leaves us there. The shutting of the womb that God so often threatens is heavy when *children are come to birth, and there is no strength to bring them forth.*

It is the height of misery to fall from a near hope of happiness. In that impassioned curse, Hosea expresses the height of God's anger: *Give them, O Lord, what will you give them? Give them a miscarrying womb.* Therefore, as soon as we are conceived in the womb our parents are right to say on our behalf, *Wretched man that he is, who will deliver him from this body of death?* For even the womb is a body of death if there is no deliverer. It must be he that said to Jeremiah, *Before I formed you I knew you, and before you came out of the womb, I sanctified you.* Eve had no midwife when she bore Cain, thus she could say, *I have gotten a man from the Lord,* wholly from the Lord. It is the Lord that enabled me to conceive, the Lord that infused a living soul into that conception, and the Lord that brought into the world that which he had animated. Without all this Eve might say, my body had been nothing but the house of death, and *to God, the Lord, belongs escape from death.* But this deliverance from the death of the womb is an entrance into the numerous deaths of this world. For when we are discharged from the womb, we are still bound to it by cords of flesh, by such a string as that we can neither come into the world nor stay in the womb. We celebrate our own funerals with cries even at our birth, as though our threescore and ten years of life were spent in our mother's labor. We come into a world that lasts many ages, but we do not last. *In my Father's house*, says our blessed Savior, speaking of heaven, *there are many mansions*. So, if a person cannot possess a martyr's house, he may have a confessor's house, because he has been ready to glorify God by shedding his blood. If a woman cannot possess a virgin's house, she may have a matron's house, for she has borne and reared children in the fear of God. *In my Father's house*, in heaven, there *are many mansions*, but, here, upon earth, the *Son of man does not have a place to lay his head*.

Why has God given this earth, then, to the sons of men? He has given them earth for their materials, and he has given them earth for their grave, to return and disintegrate to earth, but not for their possession. On this earth we have no cities, no houses, no persons, no bodies that are eternal. Even Israel has no mansions, but only pilgrimages in this life. Jacob measures his life by *the days of the years of my pilgrimage*. The apostle Paul says while we are in the body we are in a pilgrimage, and we are *absent from the Lord*. Paul might have said we are dead, for this world is nothing but a universal churchyard, our common grave, and the life that even the greatest persons have in it is like the shaking of the buried bodies in their graves by an earthquake.

What we call life is but a week of death, seven days, seven periods of our life spent in dying. Our birth dies in infancy, and our infancy dies in youth. Youth and the rest die in old age, and age also dies and determines all. All these, youth out of infancy, age out of youth arise as a wasp or serpent out of decaying flesh or as a snake out of dung. Our youth is worse than our infancy, and our age worse than our youth. Our youth is hungry and thirsty for those sins we didn't know in our infancy. Our age is sorry and angry that it cannot pursue those sins that our youth did. So many deadly calamities accompany every period of this life that death would be a comfort to those who suffer these conditions. In this sense Job wishes that God had not delivered him from the womb: *Why have you brought me out of the womb? Oh, that I had died and no eye had seen me! I should have been as though I were never born.* Not only the impatient Israelites in their murmuring *(if only we had died by the hand of the Lord in Egypt)*, but also Elijah, when he fled from Jezebel, requested that he might die, and said, *It is enough now, O Lord, take away my life.* Jonah justifies his anger toward God: *Now, O Lord, I implore you, take my life from me, for it is better for me to die than to live.* How much worse a death than death is this life, that such good men would often exchange for death! But if my case be like Saint Paul's case that I die daily, something heavier than death falls upon me. If my case be David's case, *all the day long we are killed*, every hour of every day, something heavier than death falls upon me. Though all this is true, *I was shaped in iniquity, and in sin my mother conceived me.* I was born not only the child of sin, but also the child of God's wrath for sin. *To God, the Lord, belongs escape from death.* After a Job, a Joseph, a Jeremiah, and a Daniel, I cannot doubt of God's deliverance. If no other deliverance promotes his glory and my good, he has the keys to death and can deliver me from the numerous deaths of this world by that one death, the final dissolution of body and soul.

But is that the end of it all? Is the dissolution of body and soul the last death the body will suffer (for we are not speaking now of the spiritual death)? It is not, for though it is an escape from the many deaths of this world, it is an entrance into the death of corruption and decay, of dispersion in and from the grave, in which every dead person dies over again. It was a prerogative unique to Christ not to die this death and see this corruption. What gave him this privilege? It was not Joseph's spice, which would have preserved him for more than three days but not forever. What preserved him then? Did his exemption and freedom from original sin preserve him from this corruption? It is true that original sin has produced in us this corruption. If we had not sinned in Adam, but we would have made our migration from this to the other world without any mortality or any corruption at all. But since Christ took sin upon him, inasmuch as he was so mortal that he could see this corruption, though he possessed no original sin, what preserved him? Did the union of God and man preserve him from this corruption? It is true that this method of preservation was very powerful and was able to keep him from corruption forever. He was protected by the Divine Nature itself in his body as well as soul. This Divine Nature did not depart from him but remained united to his dead body in the grave. But even with this union of divine and human natures, Christ did die. In spite of the union that made him God and human, he did not become human (since the union of body and soul is what makes us human, and the one whose soul and body are separated by death as long as that state lasts is properly not human). Thus, because in him the dissolution of body and soul did not result in the dissolution of the union of divine and human, there is nothing to make us say that, although Christ's flesh might have seen corruption and decay in the grave, his death was a dissolution of the divine and human natures. For the Divine Nature might have remained with his body and his soul.

This incorruption, then, was neither in Joseph's spices nor in Christ's innocence and exemption from original sin, nor was it in the union of divine and human natures. This incorruptibleness of his flesh is most conveniently placed in that, *You will not suffer your holy one to see corruption.* We look no further for causes or reasons in the mysteries of religion. We look to the will and pleasure of God. Christ Himself limited his inquisition in that *even so Father, for so it seemed good in your sight.* Christ's body did not see corruption, then, because God decreed that it should not.

The humble soul (and only the humble soul is the religious soul) rests itself upon God's purposes and his decrees. So in our present case Peter proceeded in his sermon at Jerusalem and Paul in his at Antioch. They preached Christ to have been risen without seeing corruption, not only because God decreed it but also because he revealed that decree through his prophets. Thus, Saint Paul cites Psalm 2 for that decree, while both Peter and Paul cite Psalm 16 as evidence of this decree. When God declares his decree in the words of the prophets, he makes the decree ours and reveals it expressly to us. Therefore, as the mysteries of religion are not the objects of our reason, but by faith we rest on God's decree, so God's decrees are always to be considered in the way they are revealed.

All revelation is either in the word of God or in the execution of the decree. When these two are joined, they are the strongest demonstration of God's purpose. When I find those marks of adoption and spiritual sonship that God delivers to me as well as the condition of obedience under which I live, I see these marks of God and so live that I may comfort myself with a holy certainty and a modest infallibility of my adoption. Christ determines himself in that the purpose of God was revealed to Him. Saint Peter and Saint Paul determine themselves in those two ways of knowing God's purpose, the Word of God before and the execution of the decree in the fullness of time. It was prophesied before, they say, and it is performed now. Christ is risen without seeing corruption.

Now this which is so unique to Christ, that his flesh should not see corruption, will extend to all who are alive at Christ's second coming and judgment. As Paul says, *Behold, I show you a mystery, we shall not sleep* (that is, not continue in the state of the dead in the grave) *but we shall all be changed in an instant.* We will have a dissolution and in the same instant a recompacting of body and soul, and that will be truly a death and truly a resurrection, no sleeping and no corruption. But for we who die now and sleep in the state of the dead, we must all pass through this death after burial, this death of corruption and decay, when the bodies that have been the children of royal parents, and the parents of royal children, must say with Job, *Corruption, you are my father,* and to the worm, *You are my mother and my sister.*

Miserable riddle, when the same worm must be my mother and my sister and myself. My mouth will be filled with dust, and the *worm will feed sweetly upon me,* and the ambitious man will have no satisfaction if the poorest people alive walk upon him nor the poorest be content that they are equal to princes, for they are equal only in dust. *One dies in his full strength and another dies in the bitterness of his soul, but they lie down alike in the dust and the worm covers them.* Even those bodies that were temples of the Holy Spirit come to this ruin, this rubbish, this dust. Even Israel of the Lord has no other name than "worm of Jacob."

After God has delivered me from the death of the womb by bringing me into this world, and from the numerous deaths of the world by laying me in the grave, I must die again in a dispersion of this dust. That the great monarch who possessed many lands while alive must in his dust lie in but a corner of that land and the private man be mingled with the dust of every highway and every puddle and pond, this is the most inglorious and contemptible vilification, the most deadly nullification of man that we can consider.

God seems to carry the declaration of his power to a great height when he sets Ezekiel in the valley of dry bones and says, *Son of man, can these dry bones live?* as though it were impossible; yet the bones did live. *The Lord laid sinews upon them, and flesh, and breathed into them, and they did live.* But in this death of corruption and decay, we see nothing that we can call man's. If we say, "Can this dust live?" perhaps it cannot. It may be the mere dust of the earth, which never did live and never will live. It may be the dust of that man's worms, which did live, but which will live no more. It may be the dust of another man, that does not concern the one of whom the question is asked. This death of corruption and decay is, to natural reason, the most irrecoverable death of all, and yet *to God, the Lord, belongs escape from death.* By recompacting this dust into the same body and reanimating the same body with the same soul, he will in a blessed and glorious resurrection give me such an escape from death as will never pass into any other death. He will place me in a life that will last as long as the Lord of life himself.

So you have the first interpretation of these words, *to God, the Lord, belongs escape from death.* Although from the womb to the grave and even in the grave itself we pass from death to death, even so, as Daniel says, *The Lord our God is able to deliver us, and he will deliver us.*

Thus, we pass onto our second interpretation of these words, *to God, the Lord, belongs escape from death.* It belongs to God, not to humankind, to pass judgment on us at our death.

The diagnosis and prognosis that physicians make about the death or recovery of their patients, they make according to the rules of their art. But we have no such rules or art to observe indications in a dying person that we would diagnose as spiritual death and damnation. We see often enough to be sorry, but not enough to despair. For God's mercies work in just moments, and many times insensibly to bystanders other than the dying person, and we may be deceived either way. We used to comfort ourselves about a friend's death if he passed away like a lamb, without any reluctance. But, God knows that his death might be accompanied by dispiritedness and disbelief and insensibility of his present state. Our blessed Savior suffered a sadness in his soul even unto death, the agony of a bloody sweat in his body, and exclamations upon the cross.

Do not come to any conclusions about any person's unwillingness to die. By his own death Christ himself has forbidden us to come to any unfavorable conclusions on violent deaths inflicted like those upon criminals. Christ had the reputation of a criminal and was executed as one, and no doubt many of those who concurred in his death believed him to be a criminal. There are scarcely any examples of sudden death found in the Scriptures, for death in battle cannot be called sudden death. But God governs by rules and not by examples. Thus, come to no unfavorable conclusions about sudden death or anger, even if accompanied with words of distrust in God's mercies.

The tree lies as it falls, but it is not the last stroke that fells the tree or the last word that prepares the soul. Still we pray for a peaceable life against violent death, time for repentance for sudden death, and modest assurance against angry death, but we may never come to unfavorable conclusions about persons overtaken with such deaths; *to God, the Lord, belongs escape from death.* He received Samson whose death is hard to interpret. Yet the Holy Spirit moved Saint Paul to celebrate Samson in his great catalogue, and so does all the Church.

Our critical day is not the very day of our death but the entire course of our life. I thank the person who prays for me when my death bell tolls, but I thank even more the person that catechizes me, or preaches to me, or teaches me how to live. There is my security, for the mouth of the Lord has said, *do this and you shall live.* But even though I do it, I will die a bodily, natural death. But God never mentions that bodily, natural death. God does not say live well and you will die well. God says live well here and you will live forever. So a good life here flows into an eternal life, without any consideration of the manner in which we die. Whether the gate of my prison is opened with an oiled key (a gentle and preparing sickness), or be cut down by violent death, or be burned down by a raging fever, I will have a gate into heaven, for the Lord is the cause of my life and *to God, the Lord, belongs escape from death.*

Now we come to the third and last interpretation as this deliverance from death is a deliverance by the death of another, by the death of Christ. Saint James says, *You have heard of the patience of Job.* In every person a miserable man, a Job, speaks. Now, says James, see *the end of the Lord*, which is not the end he proposed to himself (salvation to us), nor the end he proposes to us (conformity to him). James reminds us to see *the end of the Lord*, the painful and shameful death to which the Lord came.

Why did he die? Why did he die in such manner? Saint Augustine answers this question by saying, to this "God our Lord belonged the escape from death." What can be more obvious and more revealing than this sense of these words? The former part of this verse says, *He that is our God is the God of salvation.* So Augustine reads it, the God who must save us. Who can that be, says he, but Jesus? For that name was given to him because he was to save us. To this Jesus, Augustine says, belongs the escape from death. Having come into our life in our mortal nature, he could not leave it any other way than by death. Therefore it is said, *to God, the Lord, belongs the escape from death*, to show us that his way to save us was to die. More cannot be said than Christ says of himself, *These things Christ ought to suffer.* He had no other way but death.

So then this part of our sermon needs to be a passion sermon. Since all life was a continual passion, all our Lent may well be a continual Good Friday. Christ's painful life took off none of the pains of his death. He did not feel less for having experienced so much before. Christ did not bleed one drop of blood less at the end for having bled at his circumcision. Nor will you shed a tear less at death if you shed some tears during life.

Therefore, be content to consider with me how to this God belonged the escape from death. That God, the Lord of life, could die is strange to think about. The parting of the Red Sea and the sun's standing still are strange miracles. But it is even more miraculous that God could die. That God was willing to die makes the event more miraculous still. It is even more miraculous that God should die, must die, and "God the Lord had no escape but by death," and that "all this Christ ought to suffer." God is the God of revenge, says David, and he will not let the sins of humanity go unpunished or unavenged. This God of revenge works freely, and he punishes and spares whom he will. Would he not spare himself? He would not, for love is as strong as death; it drew in death that naturally is not welcome. *If it be possible*, says Christ, *let this cup pass*, when his love expressed in a former decree with his Father had made it impossible.

Many waters do not quench love. Christ tried many. He was baptized out of his love, and his love was not determined there. He mingled blood and water in his agony, and that did not determine his love. He wept pure blood, but this did not quench his love. He did not want to spare himself; he could not spare himself. There was nothing freer, more voluntary, more spontaneous than Christ's death. He died voluntarily. But when we remember the contract that was made between his Father and him, we see that he bore a kind of necessity: All this *Christ ought to suffer*. When shall we say that this obligation began? Certainly this decree by which Christ was to suffer was an eternal decree. Was there anything eternal before that? Infinite love, eternal love. Whatever liberty we can conceive in Christ, the decree to die or not to die is as eternal as that liberty. Yet, how minor a matter he made of this necessity and this dying.

His Father calls it but a bruise, and but a bruising of his heel. He himself calls it a baptism, as though he were to be better for it. *I have a baptism to be baptized with*, and he was in pain until it was accomplished, even though this baptism was his death. The Holy Spirit calls it joy *(for the joy set before him he endured the cross)* which was not a joy of his reward after his passion but a joy that filled him even in the midst of those torments. When Christ calls his passion a cup *(Can you drink of my cup?)*, he does detest the cup. Indeed it was a cup, a health to the entire world. Says David, *What shall I render to the Lord?* You should answer with David, *I will take a cup of salvation*. Take that cup of salvation, his passion, if not into your imitation of Christ, at least into your contemplation of Christ.

Behold how that Lord that was God could die, would die, and must die for your salvation. Both Saint Matthew and Saint Mark tell us that Moses and Elijah talked with Christ during his transfiguration. Only Saint Luke tells us what the three talked about: *They talked of his decease, of his death which was to be accomplished at Jerusalem.*" The word is of his *exodus*, the word of our text, *exitus*, his escape by death. In his passing Israel out of Egypt through the Red Sea, Moses foretold Christ's passing of humankind through the sea of his blood. Elijah, whose exodus out of this world was a symbol of Christ's ascension, no doubt had great satisfaction talking to Christ. The full consummation of all this in his death was to be accomplished at Jerusalem.

Our meditation on his death should affect us more because it is already accomplished. Can the mention of our own death be bitter or irksome to those of us who speak daily of Christ's death ("He was crucified, dead, and buried")? There are many among us who speak freely enough of death but in blasphemous oaths. Miserable men, because you have made yourselves too familiar with Jesus and may be said never to have named Jesus, you will hear Jesus say, *I never knew you.*

Moses and Elijah spoke with Christ about his death in a holy and joyful sense, recognizing the benefits that they and the entire world would receive from this death. Religious discourses should result in edification. They talked with Christ during his time of greatest glory, his transfiguration. We are afraid to speak to the great men of this world of their death, but we nourish in them a vain dream of immortality and immutability. But, as Saint Peter said, *It is good to dwell here*, reflecting upon his death. We therefore transfer to our devotions some of the steps that God the Lord made to his deliverance of death that day.

Take in the entire day from the hour that Christ received the Passover on Thursday to the hour he died the next day. Make this present day that day in your devotion, consider what he did, and remember what you have done. Before he instituted and celebrated the Sacrament (after the eating of the Passover), he proceeded to that act of humility, washing the disciples' feet, even Peter's, who for a while resisted him. In your preparation for the holy and blessed Sacrament, have you with sincere humility sought a reconciliation with all the world, even with those who refused to be reconciled to you? If so, you have spent that first part of his last day in conformity with him.

After the Sacrament he spent the time until night in prayer, in preaching, in psalms. Have you considered that a worthy receiving of the Sacrament consists in a continuation of holiness after as well as preparation before? If so, you have also conformed yourself to him. *At night he went into the garden to pray,* and he spent three hours in much prayer. I dare not ask you where you went or how you spent your time when it grew dark last night. If you spent your time submitting your will to God's will, you spent the night in conformity to him. In that time and in those prayers was his agony and bloody sweat. I will hope that you did pray, but not every ordinary and customary prayer. If your prayers were accompanied by the shedding of tears and a readiness to shed your blood for his glory, you were in conformity with him.

Have you been content to come to this inquisition, this pursuit of your conscience, to follow it from the sins of your youth to your present sins, from the sins of your bed to the sins of your board, and from the substance to the circumstance of your sins? That is time spent like your Savior's. Pilate was willing to save Christ from death by satisfying their fury by inflicting other torments upon him. But this did not redeem him; they pressed for a crucifixion.

Have you tried to redeem your sins by fasting, alms, asceticism, in order to satisfy God's justice? That is not the right way. Crucify the sin that governs you, and you will be conformed to Christ. Toward noon, they acted so quickly to execute him that by noon he was upon the cross. There now hangs that sacred body on the cross, rebaptized in his own tears and sweat and embalmed alive in his own blood. There are those bowels of compassion so revealed that you are able to see them through his wounds. There those glorious eyes grow faint in their light. The sun, ashamed to survive them, departed with this light. Then the Son of God, who was never from us, had brought a new way of assuming our nature. He delivered that soul (which was never out of his Father's hands) by a new way, a voluntary emanation of it into his Father's hands.

For though to this God our Lord belonged these escapes from death, he must necessarily die. "He gave up the Ghost," and as God breathed a soul into the first Adam, so this second Adam breathed his soul into the hands of God. There we leave you in that blessed dependency, to hang upon him that hangs upon the cross, there to bathe in his tears, there to suck at his wounds, and to lie down in peace in his grave, till he give you a resurrection and an ascension into the Kingdom that he has purchased for you with the inestimable price of his incorruptible blood. Amen.

CHAPTER V
Devotions

NOTE: *The number in parentheses indicates the original number of Donne's devotion*

1 (XVII).   Perhaps he for whom the bell tolls may be so ill that he doesn't know it tolls for him. Perhaps I think that I am recovered to such good health that I do not know the bell is being tolled for me by all those around me who see my illness more clearly than I. The church is Catholic, universal, and everything she does belongs to all. When she baptizes a child, that action concerns me, for that child is thus connected to that body which is my head, too, and grafted onto that body where I am also a member. When the church buries someone, that action concerns me. All humankind belongs to one author and is one volume. When one man dies, one chapter is not torn out of a book, but translated into a different language. Every chapter must be so translated. God employs several translators. Some pieces are translated by age, some by sickness, some by war, some by justice. God's hand is in every translation, and his hand will bind up all our scattered leaves again for that library where every book will be open to one another. So the bell that rings to a sermon calls not only the preacher but also the congregation; this bell calls us all. How much more does this bell call for me, who am brought so near to death by this sickness. The bell tolls for the one that thinks it does; he is united to God. What person refrains from looking at the sun when it is rising? But does the same person refrain from looking at a comet when it shines? Who refrains from listening to the bells that ring on every occasion? What

person is not attentive to the bell that accompanies his passing out of this world?

No man is an island, entire unto itself. Every person is a piece of the continent, a part of the mainland. If a clod is washed away by the sea, Europe is diminished, just as if the sea had washed away a mountain or one of your friend's grand houses. Any person's death diminishes me, because I am involved in humankind. Therefore, never send to know for whom the bell tolls; it tolls for you.

We cannot call this a begging of misery or a borrowing of misery as if we were not miserable enough ourselves and had to take upon us our neighbor's misery. Of course, we could be excused if we did so, for affliction is a treasure and no one has enough of it. Affliction matures people and makes them fit for God. If a person carries treasure in bullion or a wedge of gold and does not convert it into currency, he will not be able to use it to pay expenses while traveling. The nature of tribulation is treasure, but it is not used as currency, except when we get nearer and nearer our home, heaven. Another person may be sick, too, and sick to death, and this affliction may lie in his bowels, as gold in a mine, and be of no use to him. But this bell that tells me of his affliction digs out and applies that gold to me. By this consideration of another's danger I begin to contemplate my own, and I secure myself by making my recourse to God, who is our only security.

2 (IV). It is too little to call man a little world, for, except for God, man is smaller than nothing else. Man consists of more pieces and more parts than the world. And if those pieces were extended and stretched out in man as they are in the world, man would be the giant and the world the dwarf, the world but the map and the man the world. If all the veins in our bodies were extended to rivers, all the sinews to veins of mines, all the muscles that lie upon one another to hills, all

the bones to stone quarries, and all other pieces to the pro-
portion of those that correspond to them in the world, the
world would not be big enough for man to move in. Just as
the entire world has nothing to which something in man does
not correspond, man has many pieces of which the entire
world has no representation. Enlarge this meditation upon
this great world, man, as far as to consider the immensity of
creatures this world produces. Our creatures are our
thoughts, born giants that reach from east to west, from earth
to heaven. They stand astride all the sea and land and span
the sun and the firmament at the same time. My thoughts
reach all and comprehend all. Inexplicable mystery: I, their
creator, am in a close prison, yet any one of my thoughts is
with the sun, beyond the sun, overtakes the sun, and goes
beyond the sun in one step. Then, just as that other world
produces serpents and vipers, deadly and poisonous crea-
tures, and worms and caterpillars that try to devour that
world that produces them, so this world, ourselves, produces
all these in us in producing diseases and sicknesses of all
sorts: deadly and infectious diseases, consuming diseases, and
diseases made up of many individual ones. Can the other
world name so many poisonous, so many consuming, so many
monstrous creatures as we can diseases of all these kinds?
Miserable abundance and beggarly riches, how much do we
lack in having cures for every disease when we still do not
have names for all of them yet? We have a Hercules against
these giants, the physician. He musters up all the forces of
nature to relieve man. Here we shrink in our proportion, sink
in our dignity, in respect to natural creatures, which are their
own physicians. The deer, wounded and pursued, knows an
herb which, being eaten, gets rid of the arrow. The dog, even
though subject to sickness, knows his grass that helps him
recover. While it may be true that the drugs to cure him are
as near to man as to other creatures, the pharmacist and the

physician are in fact not so near him as they are to other crea-
tures. Man does not have the innate instinct to apply natural
medicines to his present illness, as do those other creatures.
He is not his own pharmacist or his own physician, as other
creatures are. What has become of man's great extent and
proportion, when he shrinks himself and consumes himself to
a handful of dust? What's become of his soaring thoughts, his
all-encompassing thoughts, when he brings himself to the
ignorance and thoughtlessness of the grave? His diseases are
his own, but he is not his own physician; though his body is
sick, he must send for the physician.

3 (XXI).   If man had been left alone in this world at first, shall I
think that he would not have fallen? If there had been no
woman, wouldn't man have served as his own tempter? When
I see him now subject to infinite weaknesses, fall into infinite
sin without any outside temptations, shall I think he would
have had no temptations if he had been alone? God saw that
man needed a helper if he was going to be well. To make
woman ill, though, the Devil saw that he needed no help.
When God and we were alone in Adam, that was not enough.
When the Devil and we were alone in Eve, it was enough.
What a giant man is when he fights against himself, and what
a dwarf he is when he exercises his own assistance for himself!
I cannot rise out of my bed until my physician enables me to
do so; I cannot even tell that I am able to rise until he tells me
to do so. I do nothing; I know nothing of myself. How little
and how impotent a piece of the world is any man alone! How
much less a piece of himself is that man! So little that when it
is clear that more misery would be a comfort to a man, he can-
not give himself that miserable addition of more misery. A
man that is pressed to death, and might be eased by more
weights, cannot lay those weights upon himself. He can sin
alone and suffer alone, but he cannot repent or be absolved

without another. Another tells me I may rise, and I do so. But is every rising an improvement? I am readier to fall to the earth now that I am up than when I was lying in bed. O perverse way, irregular motion of man, even rising itself is the way to ruin. How many men are raised and then do not fill the place they are raised to? No corner of any place can be empty. If that man does not fill the place, others will. Complaints of his insufficiency will fill it. Nature so abhors a vacuum that if it is even rumored that he is insufficient or too corrupt, another is prepared to succeed him in his place. A man rises sometimes and does not stand because he does not, or is not believed to, fill his place. Sometimes he does not stand because he overfills his place. He may bring so much virtue, so much justice, and so much integrity to the place that he spoils and burdens the place. His integrity may cast an infamy upon those who precede him and a burden upon his successor as to place a lower value on the place itself. I am up and I seem to stand, and I go round. I am a new argument of the new philosophy that the earth moves round. Man has no center but misery. There, and only there, he is fixed and sure to find himself. Every thing serves to illustrate man's misery. But I do not need to go farther than myself: For a long time I was not able to rise; at last I must be raised by others; now that I am up, I am ready to sink lower than before.

My God, my God, how large a mirror image of the next world is this! As we have an art to look from one mirror to another, and so to carry the species a great way off, so you, God, have an even greater ability to do so. We will have a resurrection in heaven. We feel that we have a resurrection from sin, and we see we have a resurrection of the body from the miseries and calamities of this life. This resurrection of my body shows me the resurrection of my soul. Since your martyrs press you with their prayers for the resurrection of the body, you will forgive me if I press you by prayer to accomplish this resurrection that you have begun in me. But, God, I do not ask, for I might ask incorrectly, nor do I beg for that which might by chance be even worse for me. I have a bed of sin; delight in sin is a bed. I have a grave of sin; senselessness of sin is a grave. Where Lazarus had been four days, I have been fifty years in this corruption. Why don't you call me, as you did him, *with a loud voice*, since my soul is as dead as his body was? I need your thunder, my God; your music will not serve me. You have called your servants, who are to work upon us according to your laws. By all these names—winds, chariots, waterfalls—you will be heard. When your Son concurred with you about the creation of man, the voice was but a whisper. There, blessed and glorious Trinity, was none to hear but you three, and you easily hear one another, because you say the same things. When your Son came to the work of redemption, you spoke, and all who heard it took it for thunder. Your Son himself cried with a loud voice twice upon the cross, just as John the Baptist, he who was to prepare the Son's coming, spoke in the voice of a crier, not of a whisperer. Still, if it is your voice, it is a loud voice. *These words, says Moses, you spoke with a great voice, and you add no more.* Not only is the voice mighty in power and mighty in obligation, it is also mighty in operation. You have given us an entire psalm [Psalm 29] to lead us to the consideration of your voice. Why, O God, don't you speak to me in that loud voice? You speak loudest when you speak to the heart. I seek your voice in your laws, but, my God, speak louder so I may hear nothing but you.

My bed of sin is not evil, not desperately evil, for you call me out of it. My rising out of my bed is not perfectly good, though, if you do not call louder and hold me now that I am up. Even they that are secure from danger will die. How much more might I, who was in the bed of death, die? As they brought out sick persons in beds so Peter's shadow might over-shadow them (Acts 5:15), you have overshadowed me and refreshed me, O God. But when will you do more? When will you do all? When will you speak in your loud voice? When will you command me to *take up my bed and walk*? As my bed is my affections, when shall I bear them so as to subdue them? As my bed is my afflictions, when shall I bear them so as not to murmur at them? When shall I take up my bed and walk? Not lie down upon it, as is my pleasure, or sink under it, as is my correction? But O my God, my God, the God of all flesh, and of all spirit, which you declared in this decayed flesh, that as this body is content to sit still, that it may learn to stand, and to learn by standing to walk, and by walking to travel, so my soul, by obeying your voice of rising, may be a farther and farther growth of your grace to proceed so, and be so established, as may remove all suspicions, all jealousies, between you and me, and may speak and hear in such a voice, so that still I may be acceptable to you, and satisfied from you.

4 (XIII). We say that the world is made of sea and land, as though they were equal. But we know that there is more sea in the Western hemisphere than in the Eastern hemisphere. We say that the sky is full of stars, as though it were equally full. But we know that there are more stars under the North pole than under the South pole. We say that the elements of man are misery and happiness, as though he had an equal proportion of both. We say that the days of man are various, as though he had as many good days as bad days. We say that man lives under a perpetual equinox, night and day equal and good and ill in the same measure. But it is far from that: He drinks misery, and he tastes happiness; he sows misery, and he gathers happiness; he journeys in misery, he walks in happiness. His misery is positive, but his happiness is problematic, for all men call misery by its name, but happiness changes with the taste of each man. My sickness now declares itself by its spots to be a malignant disease. If there is any comfort in this declaration,

it is that the physicians can see more clearly what to do. There may be as much discomfort as comfort in the declaration, though, for the malignancy may be so great that the physicians may not be able to cure it. It is no great comfort, then, when an enemy makes such a declaration and is able to pursue and achieve his goals. In intestine conspiracies, voluntary confessions do more good than confessions upon the rack. In these infections, when nature herself confesses and cries out by those outward declarations that she puts forth about herself, they bring comfort. But when comfort and confession come through the aid of medicine, it is much like a confession upon the rack. Though we come to know the malice of the man, we do not know whether there is as much malice in his heart as before his confession. We are sure of his treason, but not of his repentance. It is faint comfort to know the worst when the worst lacks remedy, and a weaker comfort to know much ill, and not to know comfort is the worst. A woman is comforted with the birth of her son; her body is eased of a burden. But if she could prophetically read his history, how evil a man he would be, and perhaps how evil a son he would be, she would bear a greater burden in her mind. There is scarcely any acquisition that does not have hidden flaws. There is scarcely any happiness that does not have in it so much of the nature of false and base money, so that the alloy is heavier than the metal. Isn't it also the case with virtues? I must be poor and be in need before I can exercise the virtue of gratitude. I must be miserable and in torment before I can exercise the virtue of patience. How deep do we dig and for such coarse gold. And what other measure do we have of our gold but comparison, whether we are as happy as others or as happy as ourselves at other times? It is a poor step toward being well when these spots only tell us that we are worse off than we were sure of before.